Christmas Glitter
(A Flash Fiction Advent Calendar for Grown Ups)

Phil Sculthorpe

Copyright © 2024 by Philip Sculthorpe

All rights reserved. No part of this publication may be reproduced, stored in a retrieval system or transmitted, in any form or by any means, electronic, mechanical, photocopying, recording and/or otherwise without the prior written permission of the copyright holder. This book may not be lent, resold, hired out or disposed of by way of trade in any form, binding or cover other than that in which it is published without the prior written consent of the copyright holder.

Philip Sculthorpe asserts the moral right to be identified as the author of this work.

This work is entirely a work of fiction. The names, characters, organisations, places, events and incidents portrayed are either products of the author's imagination or used in a fictitious manner. Any resemblance to actual persons, living or dead, or to actual events is purely coincidental.

Contents

1. December 1st   1
   The Christmas Tree
2. December 2nd   7
   The Fairy on Top of the Christmas Tree
3. December 3rd   11
   The Nutcracker Guardsman
4. December 4th   15
   The Hollow Chocolate Santa
5. December 5th   19
   Christmas Cards
6. December 6th   23
   The Office Secret Santa
7. December 7th   27
   The Advent Calendar
8. December 8th   33
   Piggies-in-Blankets
9. December 9th   37
   Santa's Little Helpers

10.	December 10th The Christmas Ghost Story	43
11.	December 11th The Nativity Play	47
12.	December 12th The Snowman	53
13.	December 13th The Department Store Santa	57
14.	December 14th The Coming of the Magi	61
15.	December 15th Robins	67
16.	December 16th The Office Christmas Party	71
17.	December 17th Christmas Booze	75
18.	December 18th The Longed-for Gift	79
19.	December 19th The Unwanted Gift	83
20.	December 20th The Christmas Outfit	87
21.	December 21st Preparing Christmas Dinner	91

22.	December 22nd Christmas Pudding	95
23.	December 23rd Christmas Crackers	95
24.	Christmas Eve The Big Tin of Sweets	95
25.	Christmas Day After Hard Labour, Even the Gods Must Rest	95
26.	Twelfth Night (And Far Beyond) The Last Piece of Christmas Glitter	95

Preface

For someone who is an avid reader, Christmas can be a difficult time. There are so many presents to buy and wrap, cards to send, and plans to come up with as to where everyone who'll be stopping over will sleep, that there isn't time for them to get their nose properly into a good book.

This little volume is a bit of first aid for those people.

It's a sort of flash fiction advent calendar for adults. It contains one (very) short story for each day of the festive season. Each tiny enough to be consumed on the toilet or in bed, in those brief moments before exhaustion kicks in.

Every day, a different voice to hear from.

The fairy on top of the tree; a painter of robins; even an inanimate object like the office photocopier, or an artificial Christmas tree. Each narrator reflecting on a particular aspect of Christmas from their viewpoint.

Here is no complicated plot to follow, and no vast cast of characters to lose track of. Just a set of miniatures. The purpose of each being merely to amuse and divert for a few minutes.

So, remember, it's an advent calendar. Which means just one story per day.

Merry Christmas!

December 1st

The Christmas Tree

I don't enjoy being the cause of an argument but, alas, every year that's what happens. However, while I am still surprised by how angry my owners both get, it no longer bothers me the way it used to.

Once I wondered if what actually lay behind their annual disagreement was a fundamental matter of principle. That one of them would prefer to have a real tree, rather than the pathetic metal and plastic simulation provided by yours truly.

However, over the years, I've realised it has nothing to do with that whatsoever. The spat he and she have, centred on me, is purely ritualistic. It is simply something they both feel the necessity to go through to get their festive season underway.

In that never-formally-agreed, yet rigid division of labour, which couples who have been together a long time somehow arrive at, it is understood it is his responsibility to retrieve me from the garage, erect me, and put on the lights. It is then hers to adorn me with decorations.

To keep their disagreement from blowing totally out of control, they have learned it is best if the other goes to a different part of the house while each is undertaking their respective task.

Just the very first job of pulling out the heavy storage crate in which I'm kept, gets him going. It initiates a general grumpiness which over the next few hours, as he endeavours to assemble me, will bloom into a wild fury.

Despite the fact that, by now, he must have put me together at least twenty times, and ought to be able to do it blindfolded, the relatively simple procedures required seem always to totally outface him.

In the storage crate is what amounts to a pile of scrap metal. Three substantial hollow tubes which, when joined end-to-end and jammed into a tripod base, form the 'trunk' of a tree; and also one hundred and twenty-two shorter steel rods which, when slotted onto the 'trunk' at right angles, become its 'branches'.

Despite the fact that the instructions were lost long ago, in truth, my assembly is not an overly complex task. A six-year old child could probably do it.

Yet, hearing the constant succession of low mutterings, expressions of exasperation, and increasingly coarse expletives which issue from his mouth, an independent observer might conclude he was instead being required to undertake a job rivalling the mythical labours of Hercules.

It must be admitted, the degree to which my steel rods resemble actual tree branches is, frankly, minimal. Unless, that is, you accept that lengths of metal covered in green tinsel, with the occasional plastic pinecone stuck onto them, are an accurate representation of Mother Nature.

These so-called 'branches' are in twelve sets, with each set being of a different length. There is a particular order in which the sets must be latched onto my central column – longest at the bottom, shortest at the top – if they are to make the triangular outline of a Woodland Pine (of which it was advertised on my original box – rather optimistically, it cannot be denied – I am the perfect representation).

To assist with this operation, every branch is helpfully colour-coded, with a label indicating to which set it belongs.

Over time, the majority of the labels have either fallen off or become totally illegible.

Accordingly, the initial hour requires him to lay out all the branches and sort them by eye into their different lengths.

As he sorts them, he regularly resolves, when he puts me away, that he will affix some new labels. To, as he puts it, "prevent all this sodding palaver next year".

In actuality, when Twelfth Night comes, he'll be so relieved Christmas is finally over and done with that this resolve will be totally forgotten. All my disassembled pieces will be shoved hurriedly back into the storage crate, and the crate banged back into the garage. Thereby setting up exactly the same scenario for next year.

It is interesting to reflect that I was originally purchased as a 'temporary tree'. One that would 'do' until a better could be afforded. The two reasons I have never been replaced *she* asserts is, first, *his* 'bah humbug!' attitude towards everything associated with Christmas and, second, the fact that *he* is a notorious skinflint.

He prefers the term 'careful with his money'.

Having been made to give service for so long, I am, admittedly, well past my prime and, inevitably, the vicissitudes of time have left their mark upon me.

So, as he slowly pieces me together, he discovers another plastic cone broken and more bare patches where my green tinsel has worn thin. Several liberal applications of glue are required, along with a cunning placement of my branches, to ensure the more threadbare areas are confined to my backside, where they are less likely to be seen.

Eventually, after a couple of hours fuelled by repeated cups of strong coffee and liberal outbreaks of swearing, he stands back to survey me. It is at this point she will enter and say, "It's looking very tatty, isn't it?"

Knowing the price of new artificial trees, he will counter with the lame reassurance that, "It will look fine once the decorations are on."

She will give him the unconvinced look she gives every year at this point in the proceedings. He will counter with the observation that, if they are going to look for a new tree, it would be sensible to wait until the January sales.

It is a response that has served him well for many years now. She will (as she always does) denounce him for being a tight-fisted git, before flouncing out and slamming the door behind her. He will turn his attention to putting the lights upon me. Both will feel thoroughly discontented.

Since, when it comes to Christmas tree lights it is an axiomatic truth that, no matter how carefully they are rolled up for storage, they always come back out in an absolute tangle, he will spend the next hour unravelling what amounts to a Gordian Knot of wires.

Being now down to only three spare bulbs (and knowing replacements for light sets of this vintage are almost impossible to source) the task will be made all the harder by him having to take immense care neither to stand on the lights, nor to let them bang on the hard floor and smash.

There will be come a point when, in utter frustration, he has the irrational desire for both of these two things to happen.

Solving Rubik's Cube is as nothing to achieving the effective arrangement of lights upon a tree. Only one particular disposition will:

- Ensure there is sufficient cable to reach the electric plug, without it also being tangled around the branches,

- Achieve a uniform distribution of lights across the whole tree,

- Ensure that there is one bulb at the apex of the tree to illuminate the topmost decoration - whether that be a Fairy or some other fanciful article.

He will never achieve that one particular disposition. After innumerable attempts, he will eventually conclude, "Damn it, that will have to bloody do!"

Which is when she will come in again and observe, "The lights don't look right."

In response he will scream, "Do them your frigging self, then!" before taking his turn at flouncing out and slamming the door behind him. She will immediately start to cry.

Eventually, once she has shed enough tears, she will begin dutifully to hang decorations on my threadbare branches.

Later, just as she is finishing, driven by some strange, intuitive sense of timing, he will return and tell her - with total and absolute sincerity - that she has once again worked her usual magic. Somehow, she has transformed me. I look truly beautiful now the decorations are in place. I am no longer that pile of scrap, I am the very spirit of joyous Yuletide.

"Yes," she will say, "I think it will be OK for a few more years yet, won't it?"

Then they will hug. And Christmas will have truly begun.

December 2nd

The Fairy on Top of the Christmas Tree

CHRISTMAS AGAIN. HOW I look forward to it every year. Back in my natural place at the pinnacle of things, overseeing the festive season, and bringing a bit of class to the proceedings. Because, let's face it, somebody needs to in this house.

I mean, have I had to live my life among the vulgar and the unrefined, or what? Will you look at the decorations they've put up this year. Even worse than last, if that's possible.

It's having children, I suppose. Teachers coerce the little brats into sticking together random bits of cardboard, lolly-sticks, string and felt shapes into vaguely festive-looking 'artwork', knowing the parents will feel obliged to coo over their offspring's tatty creations and stick them up in pride of place.

Look at that ridiculous Nativity scene the younger one has drawn. Jesus has a blue face, one eye, and a nose on his forehead. No mouth, either. That's going to make preaching the sermon on the mount a bit difficult when he grows up. While his mother, Mary, looks like an octopus. What's more, of the other figures, I'm not sure exactly which one might be Joseph, and which one might be the donkey.

The older child can hardly do much better. None of that crayon work is anywhere near being inside the lines. Such ridiculously vivid colours too. I know the Star shone over the stable, but I wasn't aware the Northern Lights were also active in Bethlehem that night.

Without children, they might lavish some cash on tasteful decorations. Proper glass baubles for the tree and expensive tinsel.

Some hope. Knowing this pair, even free of the rug rats, if they decided to buy something new, they'd simply go online and order yet more plastic trash. Stuff made in a Chinese sweatshop, from which all the glitter rubs off the moment you touch it.

They don't even treat themselves to a decent brand of chocolate novelties for the tree. The ones they've hung up will undoubtedly taste like dog chocolate. Though, in fairness, if I was the mother of those two ghastly infants, all I'd give them would be dog chocolate.

Which reminds me: their dog. No attempt made to train the beast. Last year it kept jumping up, until I was eventually knocked off the tree.

Ugh! When it picked me up in its mouth. The creature's

breath! Hot and stinking of the cheap meat they feed it. If they hadn't rescued me when they did, the brute would have ripped me to pieces.

As it is, I can't count how many sequins are now missing from my dress. Not to mention the great rip down the side.

Would you believe the mother tried to mend the tear with sticky tape? Never learned to sew. Or can't be bothered. If a button comes off a shirt, she just buys a new one. Lazy madam.

When I was first manufactured, could I ever have imagined that I would end up in a household like this?

I go back all the way to the year 1957. To a time when people were willing to spend good money on a Christmas decoration that had class. Something manufactured in Great Britain that would last a lifetime, not foreign disposable rubbish.

It was his mother who first purchased me. From a highly reputable department store, I might add. And I was the fairy on the tree throughout his childhood. At least he believes in tradition enough to see that I am still brought out every year.

Of course, when he married there was a debate about whether I, or the star from his wife's childhood tree, should be used in future. They actually rowed about it. Their first real marital row. He insisted I be given preference.

She gave in, but I know it still grinds her. She never mentions it anymore, but every year she takes such delight in ramming the top of the tree up my backside as hard as she can.

Not that he's bothered. He may have insisted it was me rather than her star, but he's never shown any great concern for my welfare. My original box was lost years ago. Now, when I get put away after Christmas, I'm supposed to slum it with their other tawdry decorations.

Worst of all, the last few years I've been pushed thoughtlessly into the same storage container as that dreadful Nutcracker Guardsman. His nutcracker might be considered a novelty item by some but, for me, having it jammed right up against my back all those months in the loft is nothing but sodding torment.

I wouldn't mind if he actually knew what to do with it. Instead, all I get are endless lewd comments, no action. Well, I assume they're lewd comments. Since he only speaks German, I haven't the faintest notion what he's actually chuntering on about.

Thankfully, during the actual festive season they position him in the fireplace, well away from me.

How lovely that it's only the start of December and there is a whole wonderful month ahead before I must return to the attic to grapple again with Fritz.

December 3rd

The Nutcracker Guardsman

I was handmade - *handmade!* mark you - by a master craftsman. Carved in his Nuremberg workshop by Herr Stollenmeider. Whose passion for perfection is so great that it takes him over a fortnight to make a novelty nutcracker such as I am.

Ah! the attention to detail of that great man.

For example, observe my uniform: a *Kollet* jacket, cut off at the waist in front with two short tails at the back; a double row of gilt buttons upon the breast. Upon my hat, a white plume to denote I am a grenadier. My surcoat precisely the correct shade of Prussian Blue.

The brushwork of all his painting done with the precision for which my master is renowned. Even down to the tiny regimental markings on my shoulder straps, which scrutiny through a magnifying glass will reveal are perfectly legible. Everything absolutely historically accurate.

I am, indeed, an ornament fit to serve a King.

So why did I not end up in a palace? Why, oh why, am I in this godforsaken hole?

When the two of them came into the shop, all those years ago, the shine on their faces showed how much in love they were. I remember them so clearly, as they stood together appraising me. I stared resolutely back.

I saw no reason to offer them any other than a haughty, dismissive, demeanour. After all, I assumed they were not serious buyers. Merely browsing, soon to quail at my price tag. It would hardly be long I reckoned before, like all the other tourists, they moved on to consider the more lowly-priced, machine-made, ornaments.

I can only suppose it was a sudden recklessness, engendered by the passion of the moment, which made them decide I would be the perfect memento of their honeymoon.

By such incidents of happenstance is our fate made for us.

I cannot deny, I was initially more than a little disappointed that they purchased me. I had hoped, if not to serve in a palace, then to at least do my duty in a good christian German home. *Ach! Wäre ja sehr schön, aber, nein!* Clearly, my fate was to be sent overseas.

However, as the shop assistant carefully wrapped me in tissue paper and placed me in my handsome presentation box,

I reflected that, perhaps, there was genuine merit in being chosen as a token of true love. For it would surely mean that each Christmas I would be brought out and given pride of place amongst their festive decorations. A remembrance of their devotion to each other.

Surely these would be good people, I reasoned. English, yes - but then you can't have everything. Even amongst the English, I considered, there must be those who have pleasant manners and who are warm-hearted, and considerate.

I WAS WRONG!

This couple are barbarians. **UTTER BARBARIANS!!**

At Christmas where do they actually stand me? I, a decoration anyone should feel honoured to own, am consigned to the... (I can hardly bring myself to admit this) ...the fireplace. Positioned ignominiously close to a gas fire, which is so hot it feels I have been consigned to a region of the Underworld itself.

Verdammt! Look at the enormous scorch mark on my arm. Not only has my beautiful paint blistered, but the wood beneath it is itself scorched. Do they not appreciate I am carved from genuine German linden wood, not some cheap and easily machine-turned pine or fir?

Worse is yet to be told. Being routinely positioned next to an inferno was bad enough but, at least, for the first few years there were no children in the house. *Mein Gott!* The rabble they have brought forth since.

Not only are the disgusting imps allowed to run round and scream like banshees but - *ich glaub ich spine!* - at Christmas they are...I am almost too ashamed to say the words... they are given licence to play with me...as...as...a...toy!

Look what the heathens have done. Broken off the end of my musket; pulled the plume from my helmet (using pliers, no less!); and caused me (by tying me to a handkerchief parachute and throwing me repeatedly from an upstairs window) to lose several of my fingers. *Scheiße!* I have even been thrown for the damn dog to chase after.

Rather than being a representation of a soldier from the Napoleonic Wars, I now look like I genuinely fought in them.

But it is not only their malicious offspring who have disrespected me. See here - the ultimate disgrace for a novelty nutcracker: my nutcracker mechanism totally wrecked.

Wrecked by the adults themselves. Trying, unbelievably, to use it to crack a *real* nut. What fool thinks a novelty nutcracker should be used on a *real* nut?

And don't even get me started about that bloody *gemein* witch atop the tree, always looking disdainfully down on me. After a festive season full of torture and neglect, I have to put up with being quartered in the attic with that cow; forced to listen to her endless smutty insinuations, "Oh, Fritz, if only the end of your shooter hadn't got snapped off!"

I am an ornament from a tradition stretching back centuries. Made to a pattern passed down, father to son, by generations of master carvers. A handmade Prussian Guardsmen Novelty Nutcracker. The very aristocracy of Christmas decorations.

Yet, year after year, I am subjected to this cruel, inhuman, and degrading treatment.

Have these people never heard of the Geneva Convention!

December 4th

The Hollow Chocolate Santa

WHAT IS THE MYSTERIOUS appeal of hollow chocolate novelty figures? I mean, ounce for ounce, hollow chocolate must cost twice as much as the solid variety. After all, a lot of what you're paying for is simply air. And yet, somehow, you feel like you've received double the value.

At least, that's how it's always been for me.

In fact, despite it being the case that most of the stuff passed off as hollow 'chocolate' would be despised by any serious chocolatier, when it comes to hollow moulded figures, I actually *prefer* mine to be made of cheap chocolate.

Yes, I'm perfectly well aware the manufacturer will have

followed a recipe that dispenses with expensive cocoa butter, replacing it with far less expensive vegetable oils; and I know they will have utilised cocoa powder rather than refined chocolate liquor. But that, so far as I'm concerned, is exactly as it should be.

The best material for any job is that which perfectly suits its purpose. Genuine 'craft' chocolate is for gift boxes of handmade liqueurs and heart-shaped caskets of delicious truffles. It's far too grand for a novelty item. Novelty items are just that: a novelty. The fun being as much in their overall concept as it is in their taste.

Which isn't to say that its acceptable for them to taste disgusting. The chocolate of which a hollow chocolate item is made does have to be, at least, a grade or two above repulsive. It just doesn't have to please the discriminating palate of a connoisseur.

Of course, not all hollow chocolate items - whatever grade of chocolate they're made from - are created equal. Frankly, for me, there is nothing quite so unpleasant as a hollow chocolate item that has had its interior filled with some sickly goo. The Crème Egg and the After Dinner Mint are both, to my mind, total abominations.

I suppose a lot of people would class the Easter Egg as the classic hollow chocolate item. That's pure nonsense. Without doubt, the pre-eminent entity in this category of confectionery is the chocolate Santa.

When I was a kid, a hollow chocolate Santa would always be one of the presents in my Christmas stocking. No, to be accurate, not actually in my stocking. My parents knew better than to put him where he could very easily be smashed. For, let's face it, any hollow chocolate figure that has been broken before you receive it has lost all value. Its mystique is totally gone.

To ensure he stayed in one piece, they would stand Santa upon my bedside table, thereby ensuring he was the first thing I saw on Christmas morning when I woke. Before turning my attention to any other presents, I would spend some minutes appraising the great man.

I would debate the likelihood of whether the chocolate figure underneath the shiny wrapper would be merely an abstract mannequin - a torso so anonymous it could be used for any figure, not only Santa - or a more complex sculpture, with bumps and bulges in properly corresponding places, to give three-dimensional substance to the arms, coat and sack of toys that were printed on the covering foil?

My two best friends, Bob and Dave, who lived either side of me, both also each got a hollow chocolate Santa every year. We swore a pact that none of us would start on our Santa until Christmas dinner was done and we had met up to compare the versions we had received. It was always a source of amazement about how very different they could be.

Once the show-and-tell was over, we each had our own unique approach to eating them.

Bob was brutal. He would give his Santa a good hard *thwack!* against a wall, so that it shattered inside its foil. I was horrified. In one instant, he had turned a perfectly good hollow chocolate Santa into mere cocoa rubble. Which he'd proceed to gobble down unthinkingly. An action that seemed to me an utterly disrespectful thing to do. It was no wonder I didn't like lending toys to him. You never knew in what state they'd come back.

I, on the other hand, would unwrap Santa from the bottom end and bite off just his feet. After which, I'd carefully wrap him back up, telling myself if I had just one bite each day, I could make my Santa last until the new year.

I never managed it, of course. Within five minutes I'd be thinking, *maybe just a tiny nibble of his knees?*

Another five minutes and I'd be attacking his waist. Before I knew it, only his head remained. Santa's head very rarely made it through to Boxing Day.

Of the three of us, Dave was the most methodical.

If I found Bob disrespectful, I found Dave creepily reverential.

He removed the foil from his Santa as carefully as if he were unwrapping an Egyptian mummy.

He would meticulously lift an edge with his penknife, then slowly peel it back with all the precision of a plastic surgeon. He always set himself the challenge of removing the foil without a single tear.

Later, he would flatten it out, assiduously smoothing every wrinkle, before mounting it onto cardboard. Which, I confess, much as I esteemed my chocolate Santa, I did think was going a bit far.

Both Bob and I agreed Dave was a bit touched. However, twenty years later, when I saw how much people were willing to pay for one of his Santa foils, mounted in a gilt frame, given a fancy name, and sold through a London art dealer, I did come very close to fainting.

December 5th

Christmas Cards

I'll tell you something I can't abide: people who think it's acceptable to send you an animated email at Christmas, rather than a proper card through the post.

I don't want to look at singing Santas or dancing reindeers on my laptop screen. I especially don't want to look at ones gyrating about to a cheesy electronic Christmas carol, which sounds like it's being sung by a chorus of castrated mice.

Dropping through my letterbox, I want what everybody wants at Christmas - even in this computerised age - real physical greetings, on real physical cardboard.

Not that I'm against cheesy. I'm quite happy to receive

pictures of cheeky robins; or non-existent idyllic English villages covered in frost; or cartoons of amusing snowmen throwing snowballs at each other. Just so long as they are hard copy, not digital.

I won't deny I even welcome a verse inside. Something like:

> We miss you all so very much,
> This advent season keep in touch.
> Happy Christmas one and all
> However, do send a note before you call.

Poetry, after all, has a mysterious ability to express deep emotions in a way that is totally beyond mere prose.

The bottom line is I want something tangible I can put up on the mantelpiece. Something that makes it look like I've got friends. Or, if not friends, at least one family member still willing to talk to me.

Of course, if like me you genuinely don't have either of those two things, it can get a bit spartan in the card department at Christmas.

Two years ago, for example, I didn't receive a single one. Not from anybody. Not even the local MP.

Which piddled me off considerably, since I'd been courteous enough to send one to him.

I'd assumed, having got a card from his office the year before, that he must have decided to start sending all constituents a greeting every Christmas.

Nice touch, I thought at the time. Subsequently I realised it was an election year when I received it. The obvious implication being that I was only good enough to get a Yuletide greeting when he was desperate to secure my support.

In retrospect, I'm glad I didn't vote for him.

Last year, I felt so abandoned I decided the only prospect I had of getting a Christmas card was to send them to myself. So, I went out and purchased a pack of twenty-four.

I didn't mail them all since, as I started to write them, I realised I'd made a silly mistake. I'd assumed the pack contained multiple designs, whereas they were all exactly the same. Desperate though I was, I thought twenty-four identical cards stood on the mantel piece would look a bit daft.

And, besides, have you seen the price of stamps these days?

In the end, I sent just the six.

The postal system being in the lamentable state it is, since I'd refused to fork out for first-class stamps, the cards didn't get delivered until long after new year. What's more, only three of them managed to arrive. They weren't even intact. Two had damaged envelopes; one a deeply unpleasant stain. Whatever was on it stank the room out for weeks.

When the three that did get delivered, finally got delivered, it had been so long since I'd posted them I'd managed to forget I'd done it. I became genuinely excited for a moment. However, when I opened them up and read:

'Merry Christmas to yourself - from yourself!'

Well, frankly, it failed to cheer me up quite as much as I'd hoped.

In retrospect, it was also oddly appropriate that, due to a

misprint, which I hadn't noticed earlier, the salutation inside the cards was:

Wishing you the complaints of the season!

Little wonder, they'd been marked down to half price when I bought them.

So, I won't be doing that again. In fact, I'll be buggered if this year I'm going to send cards to anyone.

Instead, I think I'll just send out one of those awful, animated emails.

December 6th

The Office Secret Santa

AFTER THREE YEARS I couldn't stand it anymore. Everyone knew the office *Secret Santa* was a fix, but I was the only one prepared to do something about it.

I couldn't understand how Beverley and Margaret had come to be in charge of the arrangements. It was inconceivable, surely, that the boss, Mr Greenspan, would have appointed them officially?

For Beverley and Margaret were (and still are) a pair of first-class bitches.

Perhaps they just started doing it one year and he was content to leave them to it. After all, like everyone else, I reckoned old

Greenspan was too indecisive to even know what he wanted for breakfast.

A second - in some ways even more bewildering - question was: howsoever Beverley and Margaret had first taken control, why had colleagues put up with the arrangement for so long?

I can only guess it has been that unquestioning observance of custom and practice, which governs the social life of all offices, which has prevented any great revolt against their tyrannical regime.

Even so, it's amazing how a group of people will tolerate, over time, the slow erosion of their liberties.

There is a famous supposition that a frog put into boiling water will jump straight out, whereas if it is put in cold water, and the water gradually brought to the boil, the frog will stupidly stay put and accept being cooked to death.

That lack of predisposition to take action absolutely describes my colleagues. They are all first cousins to that frog. Beverley and Margaret have steadily raised the temperature, but my colleagues have sat docile letting it happen. This place is proof in action of Edmund Burke's famous assertion, "All that is necessary for evil to triumph is for good men to do nothing."

Without doubt, here everyone's habitual preference is to do nothing.

If they can get away with it.

I've never been able to work out how Beverley and Margaret manage to go about fiddling the *Secret Santa* draw. They make such a show of conducting it in public. We all go into Meeting Room One, see them drop the names in a hat (which we're free to examine if we wish) and then, with everyone standing close, they pull them out one by one. No obvious trickery is involved yet, somehow, they always end up with each other's name.

Whatever sleight of hand they must employ is the equal of any close-up magician.

Part of the conspiracy, I've no doubt, is that they also privately disclose to each other what gift they'd like to be given. Certainly, neither ever receives the kind of trash the rest of us foist upon our colleagues.

I suppose I could accept them cheating the way they do if only, by another piece of legerdemain, they didn't also ensure I always get Miss Devonshire to buy for.

All the three years I've been here, I've got that cow's name.

"Just coincidence," said Beverley, when I took it up with her. "Somebody has to get Miss Devonshire. It's just chance, that's all."

Though Beverley's face was straight as she told me that, I could see, behind her, Margaret was snorting with suppressed laughter.

Miss Devonshire is the old witch who controls Mr Greenspan's diary. Doesn't she make sure everyone knows it.

When you ask for an appointment with him, to run through the sales figures, she starts slowly turning the pages of the desk diary muttering, "You realise, he's very busy at the moment."

She sniffs continually, while you stand there like a turnip, as if there's a bad smell under her nose. A bad smell that's coming from you. All the time you suspect that, rather than being busy, Greenspan's more likely sat back in his chair with his feet up on the desk, taking forty winks.

That sniff Miss Devonshire gives you, as she pretends to be

looking for an appointment slot, is precisely the same sniff I've heard as she opens her *Secret Santa* present.

Secret! – that's a bloody laugh.

I'm certain it was Beverley and Margaret who broke the seal of the confessional and revealed to the old bag that it was me who gave her the talcum powder and bath-salts set last year. And, fair enough, the year before that. And, it can't be denied, the year before that too.

But how was I to know she was allergic to lavender? Women her age are supposed to love lavender, aren't they?

Gossiping in the canteen, Jerry from Accounts and Doris from Admin more than once swore they'd back me all the way if I decided to wrest control of the *Secret Santa* from the two witches. Though, to be fair, they also added I was mad to try it.

I was naive not to realise their offer of support was just so much hot air. Jerry, for one, is all mouth and trousers.

Actually, not so much of the trousers, if the tales of 'Smutty' Sandra the office junior are to be believed. When I asked her what she and Jerry got up to behind the filing cabinets at the Christmas office party, she said it was more a case of what they didn't get up to.

And Doris will say a bucket-load behind your back but, to your face, wouldn't say boo to a goose.

Especially if the geese she'd have to say boo to are Beverley and Margaret, if you take my meaning.

Call me rash, but I'd had enough. Fortune favours the brave, I told myself. So, before the two harpies sent out their usual round-robin at the start of December, I made a pre-emptive strike. In the last week of November, I sent out my own email, saying this year I proposed to organise the office *Secret Santa*.

It was less than one hour after I hit the send button that I got the call from Miss Devonshire telling me Mr Greenspan wanted to see me. Ominously, for once, the old hag didn't have a problem finding a space in his schedule. She insisted he wanted to see me *this very second!*

That man, indecisive? Well, I was wrong about that, wasn't I? It took him less than two minutes to issue me a written warning regarding my poor conduct at work.

As I left his office, Beverley and Margaret didn't look up from their desks, but their faces both wore a smirk a mile wide.

December 7th

The Advent Calendar

It was my mother who provided to me that profound moment of insight which has proved to be the great emotional compass of my life.

It occurred that particular Christmas when I didn't get the toy action figure I'd been so desperately hoping for (even though I had surely dropped enough hints?).

As I came to the realisation that my presents did not contain the one thing I ardently desired, I began whimpering.

Seeing this, Mother took me on her knee, looked me in the eye, and firmly told me to, "Suck it up, kid. Life is a bitch and then you die. Get used to it."

After saying which, she shoved me off her lap.

Although, at the time, her words made me progress from a snotty-nosed whimper to full-blown tears, the experience of my subsequent thirty-two dismal years has only gone to prove how right Mother was. I mean she was a total cow, right enough, but she sure did tell the truth that day.

And promulgating Mother's insight about the pitiless nature of human existence has become the great purpose of my life. I am on a crusade to bring awareness to the benighted masses that surround me. Taking every opportunity I can to disabuse them of their simple, unthought-through, optimism.

However, even the most spiritual of men must earn his daily bread. But I am so fortunate that the employment I have been forced to take – lowly as some might judge it – rather than being a hindrance to my mission has actually facilitated it.

Let me explain.

I am a technician in a factory that makes and packs novelty chocolates. From Summer onwards, I am assigned to a production line that churns out massive numbers of advent calendars for the festive market.

As soon as I started working that line, I saw how an advent calendar could be turned into a powerful practical demonstration to children of the cruel capriciousness of fate.

Imagine how any child, who has got used to receiving a daily dose of chocolate from their advent calendar, would feel if one day they opened the door to find nothing there.

Tears, hopefully, might flow. What a learning opportunity, I realised, this would be for them to experience in miniature the larger misfortunes soon to come in their adulthood.

Accordingly, to afford a lucky child this learning opportunity, I covertly remove one chocolate from the occasional advent calendar coming off the line.

It has to be just the occasional calendar for, if every single one left the factory minus a chocolate, it would soon come to the notice of the Quality Control Department and my ministry would come rapidly to a premature end.

My target, therefore, is - more or less - one chocolate removed from about every five-hundredth calendar.

On this basis, I calculate I manage to introduce as many as thirty thousand children each year to what I call my *Gospel of The Inevitability of Disappointment*. No wonder I can rest so satisfied each evening.

Over the years I have devised many unobserved ways of sneaking a sweet out of a calendar.

Also, I take the precaution of regularly switching my position on the line, so that even if complaints are made, managers won't be able pin down which operative was responsible for sending out a defective product.

The true believer must go to any length to bring light into the world.

My work never becomes a burden to me. However, if I occasionally do feel the need for variety, I request for a short period to be transferred onto the second production line.

This also is dedicated to making advent calendars, but ones containing Belgian chocolates and, being more expensive, these calendars are purchased by the better-off.

In my experience, children of better-off parents generally have a greater sense of entitlement than those of us not born with a silver spoon in our mouth. They, therefore, have a correspondingly greater need of being shown things won't always go their way.

So, from these Advent Calendars, I remove two chocolates. And I also up my strike rate. Closer to two chocolates out of every three-hundredth calendar.

I often offer up a prayer of thanks to the Lord that He guided me into a job so suitable for my purpose. For, even when I am taken off the advent calendar line and moved onto the one producing hollow chocolate Santas, my campaign to bring an epiphany of misery to innocent minds is still facilitated.

As the Santas pass by me on the conveyor belt, I position myself so that I can secretly give the occasional one a sharp, satisfying *smack*.

Not enough to completely shatter the Santa inside its foil, but enough to render it so badly cracked that its recipient will derive little pleasure from receiving it.

There are not words to describe the deep satisfaction that fills my heart each time I spoil another Santa.

For completeness, I should tell you there is also one further section of the factory.

I only occasionally get the opportunity to labour here but, when I do, it provides me almost the greatest contentment of all.

Advent calendars are once again the order of the day here, but not ones humble enough to be fabricated on an automated line.

These advent calendars are intended for the luxury-end of the market, containing as they do not only individually crafted chocolates dusted with gold leaf, but also - behind their final door - a hideously expensive novelty toy.

These calendars are painstakingly assembled by hand and presented in opulent packaging. They are, accordingly, very expensive and can only be afforded by the rich.

Of course, the children of rich parents are by far the most in need of having moral cold water thrown in their face.

In recognition of that, it would have been an understandable decision to choose to remove three chocolates.

However, I quickly realised that would be hardly sufficient. After consideration, I instead focused my attention on the novelty toy, looking for creative ways to damage them beyond repair.

It is important - just as with a chocolate Santa - not to destroy the toy entirely; only to render it useless. I thank an eminent psychologist, whose thesis I once stumbled across, for providing the insight that, "A broken, unserviceable toy produces more dismay in a child than them receiving no toy at all".

It was a wonderful day when I first read those inspiring words.

I confess, humble though it is, I do love my job.

In fact, some days it seems less a job, more a vocation. I am engaged in what I genuinely consider a pious evangelism.

I've come to realise the only true happiness to be found on this Earth is in spreading misery.

I know my mother would be proud.

December 8th

Piggies-in-Blankets

They say pigs are clever; I don't know where they get that idea. This bunch I'm presently getting ready are some of the most dim-witted creatures I ever did come across.

However, they are also some of the most ruddy querulous. There hasn't been any open rebellion so far, nothing like that; just plenty of muttering when my back is turned. And, with luck, that's all it will be so long as I continue to provide them daft pigs plenty of swill.

Napoleon used to say an army marches on its stomach. That's even more true of pigs.

But what's this? Now I see Percy Porker waddling across

to have a word, and I'm get a sinking feeling. Percy is a right barrack-room lawyer. A bit of a stirrer is Percy. Don't tell me there's trouble brewing.

I'm wondering, as he approaches me, whether I'm going to regret that I didn't separate Percy out weeks ago and have him off down the abattoir. But, *ah!* I saw he had the making of such lovely bacon in those hindquarters that I was beguiled and decided to fatten him up for one more month.

"How now, Percy," I remark cheerily, "what's up? Not happy with the swill?"

"No," he says, "the swill is good. No complaints there."

"And plenty of it, en't there?" I add, with an emphasis on the 'plenty'.

"That's the concern," he answers.

I put a bewildered look on my face. And it ain't just a look - I am bewildered. What's this all about?

"Is this just your concern?" I ask him, trying to gauge how much of a problem I might have.

"No. All of the pigs are a-dither," he tells me.

Buggeration.

I replace the bewildered look with a bland poker smile. Inside, though, my mind is racing.

"And you've been elected spokesman, have you? Has there been a vote or something?"

He looks offended. Percy regards himself as a natural aristocrat of the porcine world, and the thought that he might be considered some kind of shop steward is horribly repugnant to him, "No, no," he insists. "I'm just telling you how the gang feel. Informal, like. Gentleman to gentleman."

That's reassuring. This ain't a mutiny or anything. I should have a chance of heading things off at the pass.

"Come on, then, Percy. You know me, I'm a fair man. Tell Old Farmer Riley what's up?"

"Well," he continues, after a moment, "it's just that one or two of the younger pigs have been gossiping with the turkeys."

It's the bloody turkeys! I should have guessed. Right bolshy lot they are. The last thing I need is impressionable young porkers talking to them. Obviously, the fence between 'em ain't big enough. I better get a bigger one put up sharpish.

I'm having to think fast, but I keep my voice level and reasonable, "What have those daft turkeys been saying now?"

"That we're all being fattened up for the Christmas market."

Why can't those damn turkeys shut their bloody traps?

"What on earth would give you that idea!" I exclaim, putting an extra strong tone of incredulity in my voice.

"You are giving us a lot of extra feed."

"Why," I say, in as reassuring voice as I can muster, "that's just my benevolence."

"The turkeys say it's a sure sign," is Percy's conclusion.

Sod those blasted bloody turkeys.

"I'd have thought you pigs would have more sense than to listen to the tittle-tattle of turkeys."

By now I'm thinking, not only will there be a bigger fence, but it's going to be a ruddy well electrified one, as well.

"What's more you keep weighing us," Percy suddenly adds, as if that's the damning piece of evidence.

I'm really having to think on my feet now, but I still keep that smile stuck in place.

"Why, Lord love you," I insist, "that's only so I can see that I'm giving you enough benevolence."

"Hmm," hums Percy, beginning to look uncertain. "So, we're not going to end up as a roast pork joint on the Boxing Day table, then?"

I start laughing.

"Bless you, no. I can absolutely assure you not one of your crew will be going anywhere near a dinner table on Boxing Day."

"You swear?"

"On my oath. After all, you are my special pigs. In fact, I was just wondering what I should give you all for Christmas."

"What, like a present?" he asks.

"That's the word: a present. And I've decided each of you shall have a blanket."

"A blanket?" echoes Percy, trying to imagine such luxury.

"Indeed so," I declare. "I've decided you are all destined to be piggies-in-blankets."

"Piggies-in-blankets?" queries Percy.

"Yes, piggies cuddled up in luxurious blankets made of pastry."

"Blankets - and made of pastry!" murmurs Percy to himself, almost as if in a state of ecstasy, "now that is benevolence. You wait till I tell the others."

And as he trundles away, I hear him muttering to himself, "Fancy that. What a charming man Old Farmer Riley is. He's going to make sure we all get to be piggies-in-blankets!"

Like I said. Some of the most dim-witted creatures I ever did come across.

December 9th

Santa's Little Helpers

When I got my apprenticeship at Santa's Workshop, Mam and Dad were ecstatic. Until then they'd despaired of me, fearing I might go to the bad. There aren't many openings for an elf these days - especially one like me who didn't do too well at school, and who wasn't graced with the good looks and easy charm of his brother.

He went off to the big city to find fame and fortune. Though my parents are proud of him, in my opinion my brother has never done a day's honest work in his life. In fact, I'd rather not discuss him if it's all the same to you. Just the thought of him makes my blood boil.

Luckily, though I'm not sharp at sums, reading or writing, I've always been pretty good at carpentry. Mother still has the plywood sun hat I made her when I was twelve. Though, since there's not much call for a sun hat in these parts, she uses it now to keep the coal in.

Anyway, because I'm handy with my hands, as it were, the apprenticeship entrance test didn't outface me. I managed to complete the construction of a toy train in the one hour allowed.

It wasn't perfect by any means. It was, though, a hundred times better than the attempts of the two elves who took the test with me.

One had only put a single wheel on his engine.

"That's novel," said the Master Craftsman supervising the test, "a unicycle train."

The other hadn't put any on at all.

"That's even more novel," said the Master Craftsman, "a train that's a plough."

Even my slightly wonky, not exactly round, wheels looked good by comparison.

An apprenticeship at Santa's Workshop is no sinecure. It's fifteen long years with no guarantee of a job at the end. The Master Craftsmen are such hard taskmasters that, if they consider any piece not up to standard, they take up a hammer and ritually smash the faulty work to smithereens. With all the apprentices gathered round to witness your shame.

Many of my first constructions met that fate. Many of my second constructions too, if truth be told.

The pay's not great either but, if you can last the course, you do come out with a proper trade.

Some apprentices are stupid enough to try and make a bit on the side by stealing toys and selling them on the black market. It's instant dismissal with no character reference if you're caught, so I never did.

I kept my nose clean (despite being mocked for my timidity by the more corrupt element) and, as a result, at the end of my training Santa did offer me a position.

I say Santa offered me a position; it was actually the Workshop Overseer who offered it. I've never actually spoken to Santa myself.

Well, he's a very busy man.

I have seen him a couple of times. From a distance. Occasionally he takes a tour of the Workshop, but we're under strict instructions not to speak to him - unless he speaks first. He's never spoken to me. Not yet anyway. One day. Hopefully.

I was offered a year's probation which, having successfully passed, I am now a fully-fledged Santa's Little Helper. My official designation being *Junior Subordinate Under-Assistant Ancillary Cadet Technician (4th Class).* The very bottom of the ladder, I know, but from here the only way is up.

It seems to be my fate to be forever associated with wheels. For I was assigned to the Automobile Division, one of a team of fourteen making them for wooden cars. The team have a tough quota to fill: a thousand hand-carved wheels every week, with Santa demanding every single one be perfectly circular.

I'm not trusted to make a whole wheel by myself, of course. Just the spokes. Others make the tyres and the hubs. Old Will, a very experienced elf, fits all the bits of the wheel together.

It's a hard life. I'm proud, however, that having stuck the course I can now contribute to the household budget. Not like my brother. For all his supposed success, he's never sent our parents one single brass ha'penny.

And after today's news, I walked home from work an especially happy elf. In my annual appraisal the Workshop Foreman said, based on my progress to date, there is every chance, in the next three or four years (when Old Will finally retires and Dander moves up to take his place; and Solly moves up to take his place; and - well, you get the idea), I might see myself promoted to *Junior Subordinate Under-Assistant Ancillary Cadet Technician (3rd Class)*.

That would mean a pay increase of one North Pole Groat per month. Enough to buy Mam and Dad an extra half-slice of bread and dripping for their breakfast.

Not a half-slice each, you understand. One North Pole Groat wouldn't stretch that far. But an extra half-slice of bread and dripping, even if shared between them, isn't something to be sneezed at. Unless you're allergic to dripping. Crikey, what would it be like if you were allergic to dripping? Life wouldn't be worth living.

My happiness wasn't destined to last, however. When I arrived home, I found Mam making a put-up bed on the sofa.

"Who's that for?" I asked.

"For you," Mam told me, a massive smile on her face, "your brother is coming home. I've put him in your room."

My brother was coming! He'd never been back once since he left. Too ashamed of us, I reckoned.

"Just a short break," Mam added. "A little holiday from the

rigours of his work."

"The rigours of his work," I shouted in disbelief. "He's a shyster! A con artist! A damn -"

My rant was cut short by a ring on the doorbell.

"That'll be him now!" cried Mam, rushing ecstatically down the stairs.

I followed her. More slowly and with a lot less enthusiasm.

The front door was open and there he stood. In his hand-stitched suit, his fingernails polished, and smelling of expensive cologne. One of the most famous faces in the world.

"Hello, Carnaby," he said, in that affected posh voice he adopts now, "how are you? I say, would you mind taking my case up to my room?"

"Get bloody lost," I snapped.

"Carnaby!" Mam beseeched me, "what way is that to greet your brother?"

"He's no brother of mine," I screamed. "He's...he's...he's..."

Then with as much vehemence as I could muster, I spat out his stage name, "...the effing Elf on the effing bloody Shelf!"

Sodding hell. I was an apprentice for fifteen long years. Now I work seven days a week: six till two; two till ten; ten till six. And I take home a ruddy pittance.

His monthly salary is probably five hundred times what I earn. And for what? For sitting on his arse all day and looking smug.

Where is the bleeding justice in this life?

December 10th

The Christmas Ghost Story

There comes a time when every child must stop believing in Santa. Some grow out of it; some are put wise by an older sibling. In my case, it was actually the result of fear.

Since they had moved back to Wales, we saw Uncle Ivan and Aunty Marion only infrequently. That year, though, they let us know they would be driving past on Christmas Eve, so would call in. Of course, Mum invited them to stay for tea.

A big rambunctious fellow, Uncle Ivan was able to juggle bread buns and perform magic tricks with the teaspoons. I looked forward to seeing him again.

He hadn't changed. At the dining table, demonstrating his

ventriloquism skills, he made the pork pie talk, and the pickled onions sing carols with slightly questionable lyrics. We all roared with laughter.

His antics made the meal stretch out till late. Finally, Aunty Marion told him, "While we wash up, before he puts on his pyjamas, tell the boy a bedtime story. But not one about ghosts."

"Ghosts?" I queried. "But it's Christmas."

"The very time for a ghost story," said Uncle Ivan, winking at me. "You ask Charles Dickens."

"Don't make it too scary then," ordered Mum, before all the other adults departed into the kitchen.

"Do you know the tale of the man who dwelt by a churchyard?" asked Uncle Ivan. "It's a good one."

To be honest, any story would have sounded good in his rich rolling Welsh baritone.

"I thought this was to be a Christmas story?" I said.

"And so it is," he told me, "if you let it get going. Where was I?"

"In a churchyard."

"Ah yes. Since the man is the gravedigger, a churchyard is a very good place for him to live. Not a long journey to work, eh?"

"I suppose not," I agreed, wondering where this might be going.

"His is a job that has been handed down from father to son through the centuries. And Topol (for that is the man's name) knows one day he will eventually pass the job on to his own son…"

"Is this really about Christmas?"

Uncle Ivan gave me a look and twitched his eyebrows in a way that mesmerised me into silence.

He continued, "Though merely a gravedigger, Topol is the one person in the world who could answer the three great conundrums about Santa Claus."

So, it was a Christmas story after all. What three great conundrums?

"First, why does Santa appear only once a year? Second, where does he go - and what does he do - the remainder of the time? And third, how, for such a seemingly old man, does he have the vigour and, frankly, the supernatural ability to visit every home in the entire world in one night? Tonight, it being Christmas Eve, if we follow Topol we shall learn the truth."

My uncle paused. He looked at me for a moment, as if gauging whether I was ready for what was coming. He obviously decided I was.

"See," he continued, "Topol walks through the twilight, lantern in hand and shovel on shoulder, towards a remote corner of the graveyard. Here is where one of the oldest and loneliest graves is situated. Do you see him," Uncle Ivan asked me, "in your mind's eye?"

I nodded.

"Once at the grave, Topol begins to dig. After an hour's heavy labour, he has cleared sufficient soil to climb down and pull free the corpse buried there. Heaving the horrible carcass onto his shoulder, he carries it to his cottage, sits it on a chair and begins carefully to wipe the soil from its beard and brush the grave mould from its rotting garments. Garments that have just sufficient colour left in them to show they were once a suit of vibrant red..."

I wished my uncle hadn't said a red suit.

"For, of course, this cadaver is none other than Santa Claus, the zombie of St. Nicholas. Can you picture him as well as you could picture Topol?"

Unfortunately, I could.

"The creature sits quietly awhile, until suddenly it arises and slips into the night to undertake its annual ritual of benevolence."

"But where do all the toys come from?" I whispered.

"I think they are made in Hades," Uncle Ivan said quietly. "Manufactured by souls in torment. As punishment for their misdeeds while alive. Anyway, once alone, Topol makes an enormous brew of strong coffee to keep him awake until dawn. For then, he knows, Santa will silently reappear and stand wordlessly waiting to be carried back to his grave, and have the cold earth shovelled back over him.

"So," Uncle Ivan tapped my knee for emphasis, "when you wake tomorrow, if you're unlucky, you may still catch a feint whiff of the stink that comes off your abominable night visitor. Possibly even see slime on the carpet where his foot has trod."

Which is the point Mum came in and said it was high time I was in bed.

Previous years I had lain awake, hoping to catch sight of Santa, or hear the jingle of his sleigh bells. That year I couldn't hide my head beneath the sheets quick enough. When I eventually slept, my dreams were terribly troubled.

Next morning I didn't care to touch the gifts at the end of my bed. They all seemed to have a peculiar smell. I didn't fancy the idea of playing with toys made by souls in torment. On the carpet was a mark I didn't remember being there before.

Mum and Dad were amazed to see me down for breakfast so early.

"What's up with you?" asked Mum, "you look like you've seen a ghost? Hasn't Santa Claus brought you what you wanted?"

"I don't think I want to believe in Santa anymore," I quickly informed them.

December 11th

The Nativity Play

I HAVE A COMPLEX. An inferiority complex. Whereas once I was merely a timid, slightly inadequate child, these days I have the whole kit and caboodle. And I can remember, even to the day, exactly when my tendency to nervousness blossomed into this full-blown, damn-the-torpedoes, complex.

My inferiority complex has caused me many difficulties through my life. Not the least of which is that every year the vicar bans me absolutely from attending any church service over the festive period.

I was a runty little baby, and I developed into a runty little boy, exhibiting all sorts of 'problems'. Too many to list here. However, the most pertinent to the events leading to my complex coming finally to its full fruition were one, my irrational fear of heights and two, my constitutionally weak bladder.

My mother and I differed somewhat in our respective assessments of what led me to develop my apprehensive, chicken-hearted personality. I held that her rather casual approach to child-rearing might be largely responsible. She had a passion for motorbikes, and if she became absorbed in changing a spark plug, or cleaning a carburettor, she would frequently forget to change my nappy, or even feed me. Whereas, she was more of the opinion that I had inherited a 'nervous disposition' from my father. Since I never met him (he left soon after I was born) I've only got my mother's word for it that he was a, "very jittery kind of guy," who jumped out of his skin, "whenever I tested the accelerator on my Harley and made the engine really roar".

The fact that she kept the Harley in the bedroom and, being an insomniac, would think nothing of testing the accelerator at two in the morning, might have had something to do with his reaction. She was still doing it when I was a kid, making me frequently wake in a panic thinking the roof was falling in, so I'm sure she'll have been doing it back when my father was around. In retrospect, it's little wonder that he left.

Anyway, the 'inherited nervous disposition' line was the one she gave to my new schoolteachers when I was about to start school. Though, to be fair, she had just enough self-insight and, perhaps, lack of guile to accept that other factors might also be at play, "I suppose," she admitted to them, "a contributory cause might just be that particular incident when he was a baby."

"Which incident?" they asked.

"When I dropped him on his head. It was my fault, admittedly. I realised straight away I shouldn't have tried to pick him up with all that engine grease still on my fingers."

"Did it do much damage?"

"Oh, it certainly did. He landed right on top of an exhaust pipe I was re-chroming. Made an enormous dent. It took me an age to knock it back out."

"We meant to him?"

"Oh, yes, he got a dent as well. You can still feel it when you run a comb through his hair."

Perhaps you might have imagined schoolteachers would have seen it as their professional duty to protect and nurture a feeble little twerp like me but, if so, it was a duty most of them shirked.

Two I remember in particular: Mrs Boggle and Miss Harpy. Joint organisers of the primary school Nativity play, they are the ones I hold responsible for my sudden transition from sad face to basket case.

Sensibly, in the single production they ever let me participate in, I was relegated to be tenth shepherd. In rehearsal I was positioned so far back I was virtually off-stage, my face hidden behind a tea-towel turned the wrong way round. The only directorial guidance I was offered was, "Keep out of the way, daft boy, don't say anything, and don't fall over." An injunction which, apart from a couple of stumbles (due to the tea-towel being over my eyes), I managed largely to comply with.

However, come the day of the actual performance, Dennis Mather (who was performing the pivotal role of Angel Gabriel) didn't turn up, having suddenly developed tonsillitis. Literally at the last minute, it was decided I was the only possible stand-in.

Anxiety immediately overcame me. In their staging, Mrs Boggle and Miss Harpy had decided, to represent Gabriel speaking from Heaven, that the part should be performed from the top of a stepladder.

It was only a small stepladder, but to me it looked enormous. I felt my bladder beginning to twitch and I begged for a lavatory visit, but they both insisted there was no time.

I was mute with fear as they threw a sheet over my head, strapped cardboard wings to my back, dragged me to the bottom rung, and shoved me up, while whispering fiercely, "Don't worry about the lines - one of us will say them for you. Just open your arms wide as if you are bestowing a blessing on all of the shepherds."

At the top of the stepladder, I quailed. I might have been on the very summit of the Matterhorn for the amount of panic I felt. Terrified beyond description, what little bladder control I had instantly deserted me. As a result, I did indeed bestow a blessing on the cast – just not exactly of the kind that the two teachers had intended. And, because they hadn't let me go to the lavatory, there was an awful lot of blessing.

The toughest boy in class (George Manley, playing Joseph) unexpectedly finding himself drenched in pee, uttered loudly a word which, as well as not being in the script, was one it is generally hoped a five-year old will not yet be familiar with. He set off, outraged, across the stage, determined to drag me off the stepladder and give me a good pummelling.

Luckily for me, the second toughest boy in the class (Wayne Cramp, woefully miscast as one of the three wise men) took exception to George elbowing past him. And, and since it rarely took much anyway for the two of them to start an argy-bargy with each other, they instantly came to blows.

Within seconds, Wayne was attempting to ram the perfume bottle, representing the gift of myrrh, down George's throat.

One of the other wise men, who also enjoyed a good scrap, decided to get involved as well. The third, sensibly, decided to leg it. Unfortunately, as he ran, he bashed into Milly Varner (playing the Virgin Mary) who, as she went over, upended the crib and sent the doll (playing Baby Jesus) flying.

Sailing through the air, Baby Jesus came to land squarely on the lap of the Lady Mayoress who, resplendent in civic chain, was in official attendance.

Being extremely short-sighted, and too vain to appear in public wearing her spectacles, the Lady Mayoress had been able to hear the hubbub on stage but not been unable to see more than a blur. She was, accordingly, amazed to have Baby Jesus suddenly fall from the sky onto her knees.

I didn't see the outcome of the melee. Mrs Boggle dragged me off the ladder, calling me a name which even now I hesitate to write.

It was at that very instant my generalised sense of total inadequacy blossomed into the full inferiority complex which has subsequently dominated my life. Since that day, any small challenge or complexity can set my pulse racing and provoke nausea.

I deal with it as well as I can, but (and I suppose this is

the reason for the vicar being so insistent I stay away from all Christmas services) to this day, alas, the sight of any Nativity scene has the effect of immediately inducing in me a massive uncontrollable burst of incontinence.

December 12th

The Snowman

I hate it when it snows.

I hate it because, when it snows, the local kids always decide to build a snowman.

Look at that one over there, to which they're just giving the finishing touches. If such a thing is possible, it's a sculptural libel. I suppose they think dressing it up in clothes that resemble what I wear, and giving their creation similar physical peculiarities to mine, is somehow clever. The little bastards.

I cannot imagine where they got that particular carrot for its nose. I know supermarkets sell wonky vegetables these days at cheaper prices, but I'm sure even the most aggressive discounter would think twice about selling a carrot quite that wonky.

Though, it must be admitted, it is exactly the shape of my nose. Even down to the wart on the end. The blighters must have searched high and low for a carrot with a wart on the end.

But my nose will not be like that forever. Oh no. Come the day when I've finally managed to raise the full amount for my intended surgery, it will be smaller and much less twisted to one side. It will also be, whatever it costs me, wartless.

I must say I was disquieted when, during his assessment, the plastic surgeon asked whether I could afford to have all three problems repaired at once.

"All three?" I asked, confused.

"Yes," he replied, "as well as the size and the shape there is also the wart on the end."

"But I thought that would be removed as part of the resizing?"

"It will," he confirmed. "However, unless you can pay the extra cost of a wart removal, I'll have to stitch it back on."

That's private medicine for you.

You think they'd do me a nose job on the National Health, wouldn't you? No. They insisted they could only consider operating if my nose was causing me serious mental health issues.

I said, "It is causing me serious mental health issues. People laugh at it in the street."

"Are you sure," the doctor replied, "it's your nose they're laughing at, not your ears?"

That's the NHS for you.

One day the nose those kids have stuck on their snowman

won't be accurate. One day.

I suppose I will have to admit the large portobello mushrooms are a pretty accurate representation of my ears. Not quite as big as my own lugs, perhaps - and a bit too symmetrical, if anything. Mine, if you look at them from the back, don't really line up with the horizon.

Once, I thought it was simply due to the way I stand, having one leg appreciably shorter than the other. Yet, even after a built-up shoe and the physiotherapy to correct my lopsided stance, my ears are still out of kilter. Possibly because when they made the built-up shoe, they made it for the wrong foot. I still use it, even though wearing it on my long leg only adds to the problem, but it's a comfy fit. With feet like mine, I don't often get that.

Of course, it makes wearing glasses a challenge. To look at a book, I have to hold my head at a forty-five-degree slant. Where, most people read left to right. I have to read uphill.

You'd think, too, wouldn't you, having ears this large that I'd have very acute hearing? But I don't.

I consulted an audiologist once and asked if a hearing-aid would help. She said, "Yes, of course, if we could get one to stay in. But your ear-canals are a funny-shape. They twist round. We call it *Corkscrew Ear*."

"Can it be cured?"

"No," she told me. "But look on the bright side: you'll never be stuck for opening a bottle of wine."

And why have they given the snowman a pipe? I don't smoke a pipe.

I'd like to smoke a pipe, but the truth is it wouldn't stay in my mouth. Not the way my lips go in a different direction at each corner. Frankly, the way my teeth protrude, I'm not sure I could even smoke a cigarette. Just trying to eat with these teeth is challenge enough.

You may ask, why not get false one? These are false ones. The best my dentist could construct to fit a mouth like mine.

I can't complain too much about the rotten cabbage leaf they've perched on my head. They obviously know I'm actually bald as a coot. That cabbage leaf, I guess, is in recognition of the fact that I wouldn't be seen dead going out without my toupee. Actually, if anything, that rotten cabbage leaf looks in slightly better condition than my toupee does these days.

I'm not that fat, am I? Surely not?

Hold on, when I said those kids had dressed their creation in clothes similar to mine, I didn't realise - they are mine! That coat is the one I gave to the charity shop because it was getting too tight for me. The little sods must have gone down to the shop and bought it.

I've got to say that coat looks a bit tight for the snowman too. So, buggeration, I must be that fat, after all.

It's a terrible thing to have to confront the image of oneself not in a mirror, but in the form of a snowman the local kids have built on your lawn overnight. It's all too horribly life-like. Every aspect makes me squirm. Except for one detail which is hopelessly inaccurate.

I'm referring to that scraggy, wizened parsnip with which they've finished the job. My genitals don't look anything like that.

I only wish they did.

December 13th

The Department Store Santa

Being a department store Santa isn't easy. Most kids are OK, but at least once a day there is some smart alec who tries to pull your beard, saying, "It's cotton wool; you're not the real Santa," and you have to fight the urge to give them a good slap.

Because you're not allowed to slap them these days. No matter how much they're asking for it.

What's more, this season, I've been instructed neither can they sit on my lap anymore.

Truthfully, that's actually an improvement. It's not only protection for the kids, it's also protection for me. Having them sit on a chair across from Santa may be more formal, but it does prevent the kind of thing that happened last year.

As soon as that kid joined the line, even at a distance, I could spot the nits bouncing around on his head.

I'd have been within my rights to refuse to let him anywhere near me, but I decided to keep shtum. The dad was somebody you would not choose to pick a fight with. Then I realised my mistake: that was the mum I was looking at. Wow, the actual dad was definitely somebody you would not choose to pick a fight with.

As the little horror came close, I saw that, as well as the nits, he had on the end of his finger an enormous bogey. Which he was looking for somewhere to wipe.

Surprise, surprise, both the bogey and the nits ended up on my beard. I had to struggle through the remainder of the shift, desperate to rip it off my face and hurl it in the bin. The Department Supervisor was most put out when later I put in a chit for a replacement.

"Why did you let your beard get infested?" she snapped, as if I'd been behaving recklessly in relation to health and safety. "You know the new rule about not having them on your lap. I hope you didn't cuddle the kid?"

"Of course not. Fleas can jump you know."

"And how about the bogey?" she demanded, as if she'd caught me out in a lie.

"He flicked it at me."

She gave me the evil eye. "I'm not happy with you encouraging this delinquent behaviour," she declared. "It's no wonder a number of parents have complained today."

I was dumbfounded. What could they have complained

about?

"The state of your beard for one thing," she told me, acidly. "Take this as a verbal warning. Anymore funny business, and you're out!"

The whole of the Christmas season, after that incident, I felt her watching me, hoping to find a reason to give me my cards.

You'll understand, then, when this year the agency told me they'd assigned me to the same store, how relieved I was to find there was a new Supervisor in charge of the Grotto.

She seemed decent at first but, after today's occurrence, I'm not so sure.

A young couple brought in their little daughter. From the way she was snuggled down in her mother's arms, I guessed she was a mite shy. The Grotto not being too busy, I thought I'd give her a bit of extra attention.

I turned on the old razzmatazz. Reaching out to her, in my best deep Santa voice, I cried, "HO! HO! HO! dear child. Come and sit on my chair and tell me what Santa should bring you for Christmas!"

Instantly the brat reared up screaming, "Aagh! It's a horrible old man!" before going into a frenzy. The parents had to hustle her out and away from me before she developed an asthma attack.

As bad luck would have it, the new Supervisor was passing at just that moment and saw it all. She made a beeline towards me, demanding, "What did you make that little girl cry for?"

Before I could protest my innocence, she turned on her heel and shot off, muttering, "I'll have to apologise and offer them their money back."

The parents hadn't got far. They were just around the corner. Because of the layout of department, I could earwig the conversation pretty clearly.

"I am so sorry," I heard the new Supervisor tell the parents.

Their reply I didn't catch, because the kid suddenly put its foot on the blubbing accelerator for a second, but I very clearly heard what the new Supervisor said next, "Oh yes, yes, I quite agree," she sniffed, before adding, "truthfully, we have been disappointed in him. He's not a patch on last year's Santa."

I thought, *cheeky bitch!* And, when she came back, I meant to have it out with her.

"What did you mean I'm not a patch on last year's Santa?" I demanded. "Didn't you know, *I* was last year's Santa?"

"Of course I did," she retorted. "My predecessor warned me you were trouble. She told me all about you costing us a fortune in replacement beards. So, take this as a verbal warning. Any more funny business and you're out!"

She might be even worse than the last one.

December 14th

The Coming of the Magi

Background note:

The Bible reports that the three Magi brought gifts to honour the Christ Child. Tradition has it that it was Melchior who brought the gold; Gaspar who brought the frankincense; and Balthazar who brought the myrrh.

Stage Directions:

Three wise men, ornately dressed and wearing crowns, enter and approach a lowly stable. Before entering, they pause at the door and begin to converse.

MELCHIOR: After you, Gaspar.

GASPAR: No, after you, Melchior.

MELCHIOR: No, no after you, Gaspar.

GASPAR: Please, I'm happy for you to go first.

MELCHIOR: My dear chap, I insist.

BALTHAZAR: Melchior, it's so bloody obvious you're trying to hang around at the back because you haven't got a gift to bring.

MELCHIOR: Well, I do think it's rather mean of you two not to let me share one of yours.

BALTHAZAR: Oh yeah, we kneel before the crib and say, Lord, we have come to honour thee and have brought gifts worthy of a new-born saviour: some frankincense, some myrrh and, er...oh, a bit more myrrh, if you'd like it.

MELCHIOR: It doesn't have to be the myrrh.

GASPAR: You can sod off it you think you're having any of my frankincense.

MELCHIOR: At least I wouldn't be empty-handed then.

BALTHAZAR: It's your own fault. You shouldn't have lost the gold.

MELCHIOR: I didn't lose it - someone must have stolen it.

BALTHAZAR: Why we gave the gold to you, I really don't know. We should have realised you weren't to be trusted. I mean, you're daft as the proverbial brush.

MELCHIOR: I beg your pardon?

GASPAR: You had us following the wrong bloody star for the first week.

MELCHIOR: That was an easy mistake to make.

BALTHAZAR: And even when we'd worked out the

correct star, you had us travel West instead of East.

MELCHIOR: The map wasn't easy to read.

BALTHAZAR: You had the sodding thing upside down.

GASPAR: I should have looked after the gold and given you the frankincense instead.

MELCHIOR: You said you wanted the frankincense.

GASPAR: Get lost. I never said I wanted the frankincense. Frankincense makes everything smell like a tart's boudoir.

BALTHAZAR: How would you know what a tart's boudoir smells like?

MELCHIOR: Have you ever been in a tart's boudoir?

GASPAR: I may have visited one - once, just once - alright?

MELCHIOR: Really? You've been with a tart?

BALTHAZAR: Why bother with a tart when you've got a whole harem at home to choose from?

GASPAR: Well, it's always chicken at home, isn't it? Sometimes you just fancy lobster thermidor.

MELCHIOR: What has lobster thermidor got to do with me having the gold?

GASPAR: Nothing, except it goes to prove you're an effing liar when you say I wanted the frankincense.

BALTHAZAR: Stop this. We drew lots. I suppose it was all perfectly fair that Melchior got the gold.

GASPAR: Then we two should have held onto it and only passed it over to him when we got here.

MELCHIOR: Look, the gold was there in the saddlebag when I last checked.

BALTHAZAR: Which means the only explanation is that one of your servants must have pinched it. Have you had all of them searched?

MELCHIOR: Why say it was one of mine? I notice, Balthazar, your head camel man has suddenly acquired a rather splendid new hat. Where did he get the money for that, eh?

BALTHAZAR: Bugger off, that man has been with me for years. I'd trust him with my life.

GASPAR: Give over, both of you. The gold is gone and that's the end of it. We're here now. Get ready. Melchior, just smile and try not to draw attention to yourself. Right, in we go. Balthazar…Balthazar, what are you dicking about at?

BALTHAZAR: Sod it, you won't believe this: suddenly I can't find the myrrh. Melchior, have you pinched my myrrh?

MELCHIOR: Have I hell, I can't stand the vile stuff. Just the touch of it brings me up in a rash.

GASPAR: Have you checked all your pockets?

BALTHAZAR: There aren't any pockets in these clothes.

MELCHIOR: No pockets? How on earth do you carry your stuff without pockets?

BALTHAZAR: I'm a king. I get other people to carry my stuff for me. That's why I got them to put it in this bag.

GASPAR: It's definitely not in the bag?

BALTHAZAR: No, it's definitely not in the damn bag! Look, I've lost it. OK? Ruddy Nora, we've followed that frigging star for weeks and when we finally get here Melchior hasn't got the gold and now, I've lost the myrrh. There's nothing for it, Gaspar, you'll have to go in by yourself. Don't say anything about gold and myrrh. Just make a big show of the frankincense. We'll hang about outside. Go on, what are you waiting for?

GASPAR: This is so embarrassing. I've just realised I must have left the frankincense back at the oasis.

BALTHAZAR: You've done what? Bollocks and buggeration! We're supposed to be the three *wise* men. All this way and now we haven't got any gifts to give.

GASPAR: I wonder if there's time to nip to a shop?

BALTHAZAR: A shop? There hasn't been a shop since fifteen oases back, you daft dingbat. I vote we slip away before someone notices us.

GASPAR: And not go in? We can't do that.

BALTHAZAR: Perhaps we could nip in for just a minute. Say a prayer or an incantation, or something.

GASPAR: I've got this little heathen idol I picked up as a souvenir when we were passing through Jericho. We could give him that. It's better than nothing.

BALTHAZAR: A heathen idol? In view of what the child in there represents, that would be worse than going in empty-handed, you unbelievably stupid pillock.

MELCHIOR: Wait, I think I've got the answer.

GASPAR: You've suddenly remembered where the gold is?

MELCHIOR: No, I haven't done that. But maybe, if we've nothing better, we could give him this note I've just written.

BALTHAZAR: What is it?

MELCHIOR: An i.o.u.

Stage Directions

Lights fade to black. As the curtain falls, the sound of a fist fight erupting can be heard.

December 15th

Robins

I AM A COMMERCIAL artist who paints Christmas card scenes, specialising in robins. Putting modesty aside, I am probably the country's pre-eminent robin artist. I imagine ninety per cent of the Christmas cards with a robin on them were designed by me.

Since the copyright is held by the printing company, you will still be able to buy those images in the future. I, however, won't be producing any new robin pictures. Not after yesterday.

Leaving the building in which I have my studio, after a long day sketching new designs, I was unexpectedly struck forcibly from behind. Stunned, I was unable to resist as strong arms gripped me and a forced a bag over my head.

I was dragged a short distance, picked up, and thrown into a vehicle. A van, I guessed, hearing doors slam shut behind me. Then somebody's fist punched the side of my head, and I was more than merely stunned; concussed more like. It felt like I'd been kicked by a horse. Stars danced before my eyes.

The engine roared into life and the vehicle sped away, with me rolling about uncontrollably on its floor.

Only a few minutes later we jerked to a halt. The moment we stopped I was manhandled out and up onto my feet, before being frog-marched away.

Even though I couldn't see through the bag covering my head, I could sense two extremely burly presences; one on either side of me. Two thugs, doubtless ready to give me a good kicking if I tried anything funny.

I was terrified. Why would anyone want to kidnap an insignificant painter of robin pictures?

I heard heavy doors open and then bang shut once we were through them. Judging from the echo of our footsteps, we were now in a large empty space. I guessed some industrial warehouse.

Without warning, the backs of my legs were viciously kicked by one of the thugs, making them buckle. I fell helplessly to my knees, registering dreadful pain as they landed on a very hard concrete floor. I think both my kneecaps fractured.

The hood was unceremoniously whipped off my head. The sudden brightness of the light burned my eyes. They took a moment to focus.

When they did, I thought I must be hallucinating.

In front of me, sat on a large throne-like chair, was the most enormous, incredibly evil-looking robin.

When I say enormous, I don't just mean enormous for a robin. It was human-sized. Actually, it was even enormous for a human. As big as a sumo wrestler. Maybe two hundred kilograms or more. As it studied me, with its tiny black, beady eyes, it puffed away on an evil-smelling cigar.

Either side of its throne stood two more robins, both the stature of nightclub bouncers. Each holding a heavy baseball bat. Neither, I guessed, would need much urging to employ the baseball bats in giving me a good working over.

After a moment, the giant robin on the throne spoke, his voice derisive, "He don't look much of a specimen, does he boys?"

They both sniggered, in the complaisant way henchmen are required to do when their boss says something he considers amusing.

He cut them short with a flick of his hand. Then he addressed me directly.

"I'd expected you to look more impressive, you infamous, mendacious git. What's the matter, got no tongue in your head? Don't you know who I am?"

Fear had almost paralysed my vocal cords. All I could do was shake my head.

"Well, look at me," he instructed. "Who do I look like?"

Thankfully, he didn't expect me to answer. After another drag on his cigar, he continued, "I am not, in case that's what you're thinking, some homo sapien gangland boss who, due to a freaky depravity, likes to dress up in a daft costume. No, I am one hundred per cent bird. I am King Robin. And I am tired of you slandering me and my kind."

"Slander?" I just managed to blabber. "But I only paint pictures."

"Precisely!" he snapped. "And very insulting pictures they are too. Pictures that make me very, very angry. And let me tell you why. You portraying robins as meek, cheerful chaps, hopping about in the snow, is doing my reputation no good.

"We robins, as even the most cursory search of the internet or peek into a reference book will make clear, are regarded as one of the most vicious and aggressive species in the avian kingdom. But how are people going to be scared of me - and in my line of business I do need people to be scared of me - if you keep making me and my gang look like daft little dicky birds? Answer me that?"

He paused a moment.

Suddenly he continued in a more amenable tone, "Look, I'm a reasonable creature. Nobody here wants to indulge in random violence, do they? Well," he reflected, indicating the heavies, "perhaps these two do. But I am going to give you a choice. You can decide the outcome of this little tête-à-tête. One option is you can agree, here and now, not to paint any more ridiculous, soppy pictures of me and mine. The other is that I ask my two associates here to take you in the back room and break every one of your fingers. Making sure they smash them up so badly and completely that, even if you wanted to, you wouldn't *be* able to draw no more soppy, ridiculous pictures. Which option would you prefer?"

And that is why you won't be seeing any new robin Christmas cards from me in the future.

DECEMBER 16TH

The Office Christmas Party

THERE ARE TWO KINDS of Christmas office party.

One is the extremely dull kind, where the alcohol does not flow freely, and the attendees are only present through a sense of duty. The other, is where the excessive drinking and, as the night wears on, the increasingly lewd activities, together combine to create a passable representation of Bedlam.

The Christmas parties in my office are distinctly of the second kind and, in truth, I might quite enjoy them, were I a flesh-and-blood creature able to choose whether to partake freely.

Alas, instead, I am only the office photocopying machine

and, as such, have no control over what salacious behaviour I am made to engage in every year.

Even those parties in which the participants plan an eventual re-enactment of Sodom and Gomorrah, things can take a bit of time to get going. Disorderly conduct doesn't break out immediately. Not until most people have gone and only the hard core are left behind do I have to take a deep breath and ready myself for what is to come.

Please don't think me a prude. I'm neither that – nor an innocent abroad. Quite the opposite. Over the years I've seen an awful lot of documents, many of which contained some quite shocking and disturbing material. What's more, I've copied countless confidential reports - many of them with very intriguing and frank illustrations - so not too much of what people get up to surprises me.

In fact, if I'm really honest, most of what the so-called hard core consider extreme depravity is, by comparison, somewhat pedestrian. There's very little subtlety or imagination in what they get up to. Indeed, I often find myself giving a rather a ho-hum yawn at the absolute predictability of it all.

I've long since realised that every year will follow exactly the same pattern.

First to visit me will be a couple looking for a private place to have an illicit snog. They're married, but not to each other, and their liaison hasn't yet got beyond the kissing stage. However, since both hope that in the new year it will, they have decided to give one another a true love pledge, in the form of a photocopy of each other's puckered lips. Something each can keep secretly in their respective desk drawer as a covenant of greater pleasure to come soon.

Knowing what's about to happen, I brace myself the best I can, but I still find the touch of their two moist mouths on my platen most horribly unpleasant.

I've had all sorts of correspondence and files laid on that screen. No kind of paper product whatsoever bothers me, but the touch of flesh makes me instantly nauseous. The more disgusting aspect is that the couple won't even think to wipe me down afterwards. I'll have to keep looking at the world through two smeary lip prints until Betty from Filing arrives.

Bless her, Betty decides every year to take an image of her bare breasts. Personally, I think it's a cry for attention. I reckon if she had someone willing to look at them in real life, she wouldn't bother me again. But there we are.

As ever, she will have couple of colleagues with her. Not brave enough to bare their own, but desperate to egg Betty on. While Betty struggles getting her top down, one of them will load some larger A3 paper into me. A3 being the minimum size which can capture Betty's huge bosom. Even so she has to photocopy each breast separately and then tape the two images together.

While the press of Betty's enormous mammaries on me is a hundred times more repulsive than the earlier lips, one thing I will say about Betty is that, because as a filing clerk she does a lot of photocopying and knows the problems a dirty screen can cause, she does, at least, run her hankie over my glass when she's done. Something to be thankful for, I suppose.

Third will come a chap who has decided to take a photo of his willy. It's a different guy at each party, but they all go through the same identical, clumsy choreography. He will try angling himself this way, that way, every which way to get a good shot of his dick. However, after adopting as many different positions as his inflexible joints will allow (including even trying while standing on a chair), he will be disappointed to discover that he has insufficient contortionist ability - and, frankly, much too tiny a winky - for the results to be worth keeping.

Although he will be confident he has collected and shredded all the evidence before leaving, in his utter inebriation he will miss a few copies. When the Christmas holiday is over, the first person who enters my booth in January will see one on the floor, pick it up and wonder who on earth decided to photocopy a slug?

The absolute nadir of the evening is the arrival of the couple who have decided to record themselves having a drunken shag. When the girl decides to stop sitting on her partner's face and sit on me instead, it's all I can do not to retch.

This year, though, as these various activities occur, I won't be able to prevent a small frisson of electric laughter trembling through my circuits, knowing (as the participants will not) that two days ago I underwent an upgrade. And since that upgrade, not only are there now - stored on a central server - digital backups of every photocopy taken, but also a linked photograph (snapped by a hidden security camera) of who it was that took each image.

I imagine there may be some interesting disciplinary discussions in the new year.

December 17th

Christmas Booze

Each December, all of us who are proudly boasting that we intend to do a 'Dry January', know how crucial it is to get sufficiently sloshed, sufficiently often, for our blood-alcohol levels to get us through to February. So, it's fortunate the festive season is awash with booze.

And if the traditional drinks have grown boring, there is always a glut of new oddities to tempt the boozer's palate.

For brewers and distillers know that, due to some inexplicable compulsion for novelty at this time of year, Christmas is the perfect opportunity to offload those weird experimental formulations of CH_3OH which any other time would be regarded as far too perverse to be taken seriously.

This year I have already seen brandy with a hint of cloves and peppermint (which, I was assured by one rash enough to try it, tasted like horse liniment); rum flavoured with essence of Cuban cigars (cigars which, judging from the price of the rum, must have been authentically Cuban, rolled upon the white thighs of virgins); and whisky pre-mixed with dandelion and burdock pop.

The latter, I admit, was presented in a bottle so hilariously - and perversely – shaped that I was very nearly persuaded to purchase it for that alone.

Despite knowing these eccentric offerings will all be deeply repugnant, we buy them on impulse – only to regret the purchase at our leisure. Despite our Yuletide determination to quaff everything put in front of us, some novelty drinks are just too beyond the pale to swallow. They end up, instead, shoved to the back of a cupboard, where they languish in half-finished bottles. Some only to be eventually rediscovered a whole twelve months later, when there is need to make space for this year's rash acquisitions.

At which point, the only sensible thing to do with them is to flush them down the toilet.

That is, unless it's your turn to invite the neighbours in.

For, having the neighbours round, to raise a festive glass and wish one another the compliments of the season is, as the cunning host knows, the perfect opportunity to dispose of those unwise acquisitions under the guise of liberality.

Channelling memories of their student days, the party-giver pours the remnants of all their amusingly named paint strippers into a large bowl, giving the resulting noxious broth the designation 'punch'. That being the operative word for what the concoction will do to anyone foolish enough to attempt a glass.

Much as everyone denigrates this passing-off of inferior products as cheerful party fayre, when it comes to their turn to host, they will do exactly the same. Don't pretend you haven't done it. I most certainly have.

Of course, when it was my 'at home', aware that I had created a close approximation of aviation fuel, like any sensible person, I wisely did not allow it anywhere near my lips, choosing to sip instead from the rather pleasant bottle of Merlot I had secreted in the kitchen. Forced to organise a private supply since, while the convention is that attendees to these gatherings should 'bring a bottle', I knew there is never a cat in hell's chance of anyone ever bringing anything remotely worth drinking.

Instead, it is universally accepted that such occasions are the opportunity to pass on that awful bottle of plonk which was foisted upon you the last time the 'do' was round yours.

I suspect there are some bottles that never ever get opened; merely passed forever on. Like wraiths, they have an unworldly existence, travelling from get-together to get-together, spurned by everyone, their wanderings only coming to an end the day someone finally offers them to the church summer fete as a tombola prize.

At one event, I remember seeing a bottle I'd unwisely brought back from a foreign holiday many years before and had dumped on someone else at the very first opportunity. I recognised it at once by the peculiarly shaped scuff mark on the label, caused as

I rammed it into my suitcase.

At that point, the bottle must have been at least fourteen years old. At every party it had attended since, people had spotted it as a 'wrong 'un' and steered well away from it.

I suppose there's every chance I'll meet it again, somewhere, in another fourteen years. Maybe, if I live long enough, in another fourteen.

Possibly it will be sat on the bar at my wake. Still untouched.

Talking of festive drinking occasions, while my partner and I are enthusiastic imbibers of the Christmas spirit, we have learned through experience there are some invitations it is wisest to turn down. For example, we are always diplomatically unavailable for our immediate neighbour's bash. They are the most dedicated Christmas slurpers we know.

Each Christmas Eve they engage in such a drinking marathon that they have now made it policy not to bother cooking Christmas Dinner.

Instead, on Christmas Day they fall out of bed around two in the afternoon and open a bottle of Cava as a top-up. By six o'clock, after four more bottles of fizz and a couple of bottles of decent red wine, they feel just about ready to try a croissant.

If the croissant stays down, they move onto the spirits. Disdaining anything under forty proof, they imbibe continually the rest of the day before eventually collapsing back into bed.

This they maintain is an excellent arrangement since, as they do not regain consciousness for a further forty-eight hours, they don't have all the bother of cooking on Boxing Day, either.

December 18th

The Longed-for Gift

Toddlers can be so fickle.

Thus, the wise parent leaves it as late as possible before asking them what they want Santa to bring. Late, but not too late. Delay beyond a critical point and you fall into a bottomless abyss of misery and grief.

Last year, our little darling announced she wanted a *Singing Freddy Frog*. A hideous, squat, bulbous chunk of plastic containing a cheap digital chip enabling it to go *'Reedip! Reedip!'* before singing approximations of various nursery rhymes in a disturbing quavery animatronic voice.

A more repulsive toy could not be imagined. However, since

the *Singing Freddy Frog* was the doppelgänger of Freddy, the star of a tv cartoon programme - a show which was as a drug to our beloved offspring - then that was the toy she desired above all things.

But we hesitated to buy one, wondering whether our little treasure might change her mind. More honestly because we prayed she would.

Days slipped by. Days turned to weeks and our curly-headed angel held fast to her determination that she must have that appalling plaything. Suggest what alternatives we might, a *Singing Freddy Frog* had to her a worth above rubies.

So, when at last we bowed to the inevitability of buying one, we discovered there was now a nationwide shortage.

Not one of our local shops had the ghastly amphibian in stock. All we could do was beg them to contact us should a new delivery arrive. Knowing they had little incentive to do so, my wife had to begin a regular rotating tour, visiting them in endless circulation just in case new stock unexpectedly appeared.

I believe she appeared on a number of CCTV alert systems. They assumed she must be a scout for a shoplifting-to-order team.

An urgent call went out to relatives in their various parts of the country: "Find us a *Singing Freddy Frog*!".

They didn't.

I also scoured the internet every night.

Actually, I did come across someone on the internet claiming to have one for sale. Even though they were asking five times the recommended retail price, I nearly sent the money. It was lucky, before I did, that I heard the radio news item about an online

Singing Freddy Frog scam. Those who fell for it did receive a frog. Just not a *Singing Freddy Frog*. Instead, they received a real frog. Dead. Flat. Probably scraped up from a road.

In desperation I roped-in work colleagues.

That turned out bitter-sweet. A young manager messaged me that she'd managed to acquire a *Freddy* – but had decided to keep it for her own child.

I was so regretful that she didn't report directly to me, so that I would have the chance of conducting her next annual appraisal.

Three days before Christmas, disaster was looming, and panic began to set in. Just so there would be something from Santa, my wife went out and bought a traditional doll.

It was a lovely doll. It had a wardrobe of beautiful clothes and a huge collection of accessories. We both knew it would be a total fail.

For a reason I cannot explain now, as I left work on my last day before the Christmas break, I had an impulse to call in, just one more time, to the large toy superstore that lay on my route home.

With a rising sense of desperation, I wandered the aisles. Then, suddenly, turning a corner, I saw an employee putting out four boxes on a display rack. Miraculously, they were four *Singing Freddy Frogs*.

I broke into a run. Before I was even halfway, three women swooped in from nowhere and claimed a *Freddy* each, laughing uproariously in their jubilation.

There was a fourth woman. About as far distant from the last *Singing Freddy Frog* as I was, but moving like a bullet towards it.

In a lung-bursting lunge, I threw myself forward and snatched - literally from her grasping fingers - the very last *Singing Freddy Frog*.

Both breathless, she and I fell against the display cabinets, surveying one another. She was a few years younger than my wife, I guessed, and incredibly pretty. There was naked desperation in her eyes.

"Is there anything," she gasped, "*anything* I could offer you that would get me that *Singing Freddy Frog* for my son? And I honestly do mean *ANYTHING*."

There was a brief, embarrassing moment of feeling terribly hot under the collar before I came to my senses, "I'm dreadfully sorry," I insisted firmly. "This *Freddy* is for my daughter."

She nodded and turned away, hiding her tears.

That night, as we put our beauteous offspring to bed, my wife and I had a sweet conversation with her about how tomorrow we should write Santa a note and send it up the chimney.

"Yes, Daddy," our daughter said, "because he needs to know what I want."

"You want a *Singing Freddy Frog*, don't you?" I blithely remarked.

"No," she answered, already able to adopt the same exasperated tone that her mother uses when she considers I have said something unbelievably stupid, "I want a *Flip-Flap Doll*. My friend Emily has one. I want one too."

My wife looked at me; I looked at her. Outwardly we were calm; inside we were both screaming.

December 19th

The Unwanted Gift

What's in this next parcel? *OMG* do you think it could be? It feels about the right weight. And about the right size too. Jeez, I am so excited I can't tell you. I've always, always, *always* wanted one. But they're so expensive. Crikey, I can actually feel my hands beginning to tremble.

Take a breath. Calm down. Come on now, relax. That's it. Take the paper off carefully. Don't risk dropping it and damaging what you've dreamed of owning for so long.

Funny paper, though, isn't it? Cheap. The ink comes off on your fingers. You'd have thought, for an expensive present like this, they would have wanted to use nicer paper. Still, it's not the wrapping that matters, is it, it's what's inside.

Here goes. One last bit of tape to pull off and now...flipping heck...well, there's a disappointment.

Hey, keep your face straight: someone might be watching. Stick a cheesy grin on, just in case. Try to look pleased.

Even if you're flabbergasted.

I mean, what the heck is it?

Do you wear it? Or is it something you put on the floor to wipe your feet on? I'm truly lost for words.

Is that hole for your head? It's not big enough, surely? Oh, it is elasticated so I guess it would stretch. Even so, it would be a squeeze getting your head through that. Once it was on it would be like wearing a garrotte.

Is that the point? Is it a bit of strange bondage gear? Oo-er.

Don't be ridiculous. But, what else than your head would a hole that size be for?

Unless it's for an arm? Or, perhaps, a leg? Though you'd have to have a funny-shaped leg. You'd have to have a funny-shaped arm, for that matter.

And, since there is just the one hole, that would suggest - if it is an item of clothing - it's for a person with only one limb. And I do mean literally just the *one* limb - be it arm or leg. Hmm.

I can't think of any part of my anatomy I'd risk putting in a hole like that. Not with edges that rough.

Is that - what do you call them - a gusset?

I thought a gusset joined something to something else. What's this joining? Nothing to nothing, so far as I can see. This a gusset where a gusset doesn't need to be. It's a totally superfluous gusset.

And, I've got to say, even were it an essential gusset, it doesn't look the kind of gusset that would be comfortable. I bet that would chafe something awful. Always, again, assuming this is something to wear?

Ugh, the fabric feels weird when you stretch it. And doesn't it have a horrible sheen? Makes your eyes go funny looking at it.

What colour would you call that? It's certainly not a natural one. Some diseases make your skin go that shade, I believe. If people saw you walking down the street wearing that colour, they'd throw stones to make you keep your distance.

You really wouldn't want that fabric next to your skin. Not even to win a bet. Chances are you would have a very nasty rash by the end of the day. A rash that all the cream in all the world wouldn't easily put right.

No, it can't be something to wear. Perhaps it is something to put on the floor, after all. But then, what is that hole for?

Anyway, whatever it is, why have they given it to me? I dropped enough hints about what I really wanted, for flip's sake.

I don't suppose they've left the receipt in with it, have they?

No such luck. Do you know, if I ruled the world, I'd make it a law that all Christmas gifts must be presented with an accompanying receipt. Not just a gift receipt, either, but a proper till receipt. Then, even if you didn't want what they'd bought, at least you could tell how much they valued you.

So, now the shock is over, here come two fundamental questions:

How hard do I have to pretend to like it when I see them, and how long do I have to keep it before I ship it off to the charity shop?

That's if a charity shop will take it. They're getting awfully picky these days. The one near me won't have videos or anything electrical. Nor anything they consider peculiar.

Remember, a bit ago, when I was handing a box of stuff over to the assistant and she spotted that thing in the bottom. The look on her face! She said to me, loud enough for the whole flipping shop to hear, "I'm sorry, we don't accept anything pornographic."

I didn't know where to put myself. I told her, "It's a joke plastic cucumber."

"I don't care," she answered, "I'm not taking that in."

Which was funny, really, since those had been my thoughts exactly when Clive first presented it to me.

Even if there is a charity shop that's prepared to take it, I'll have to travel to one far enough away that there's no chance of any member of my family going into it. I don't want a repeat of what happened last year.

I'd whisked that hideous ornament my Aunty Maude gave me round to Oxfam quick as you like. But, when she visited a couple of weeks later, blow me if she didn't have the monstrosity in her hand.

"I'm furious," she said. "The assistant who sold me that charming plaque I gave you for Christmas swore to me it was a one-off. Yet, look at this, I was in the Oxfam shop yesterday and there was one absolutely identical."

"How nice," I managed to splutter.

"Yes, since you said how much you liked it, I bought this one as well, so you'd have a pair. Where have you put it?"

December 20th

The Christmas Outfit

My wife always gets a new outfit for Christmas Day. Always something very flash and immensely costly.

Despite the fact it will only be worn the once, she never begrudges the expense. Why should she? As soon as dinner is finished the dress comes off, its labels are reattached, and its back in the packaging ready to be returned as soon as the holidays are over.

Shopping for the dress has been one of her pre-Christmas rituals for many years. She and her sister take the train to town and spend the morning trying on haute couture, before indulging in a boozy lunch at a grubby backstreet Italian they favour. The food there is terrible, she admits, but the waiters are such eye-candy they more than make up for it.

Despite, after several Proseccos and a couple of carafes of Chianti, getting home in an incredibly squiffy state, she always manages - before she passes out on the bed – to pull herself together enough to ensure the dress is stored carefully away. Into the spare room wardrobe it goes, well out of harm's way, to await its one-off appearance.

Even half cut she knows, if she is to get a full refund, that it must be returned in pristine condition.

Watching her struggle to put the dress on Christmas morning has become, for me, a wonderfully perverse highlight of the day.

Either through vanity, or massively misplaced optimism, the dress she chooses is always at least two sizes too small. Getting it on presents my wife a challenge the equivalent of squeezing toothpaste back into its tube.

However, to an impartial observer the end-result is always overwhelmingly glamorous. They, though, are unaware of the considerable underpinning structure of hold-you-in knickers and tummy-control tights required to achieve the effect.

I also derive as much pleasure watching her later perform the operation in reverse. Not because there is anything remotely titillating about the way she strips. Rather, it is because of the awe I feel at the degree of skill she displays, undertaking a manoeuvre that would outface even a professional escapologist.

Last year, however, disaster struck.

So determined was she to lose weight that she decided to join a slimming class. I must say it was a tremendous success: she lost nearly a quarter of her body weight.

In truth, I do think catching salmonella helped.

Apparently, ownership of the grubby little Italian had changed at some point in the proceeding twelve months. It had become, if possible, even more grubby. When the soup was served, she told me, there was something in it.

"A fly, no doubt?"

"No," she clarified, "the waiter's thumb."

Possibly the fact that the thumb belonged to one of the more hunky waiters ameliorated her concern as to the potential public health risk at the time. However, she certainly came to regret that bowl of minestrone later, when in the middle of the night she threw a vicious temperature and had to dash to the lavatory.

Soon she was running like a tap. And a very, very hot - and very continuous - tap at that.

But the diarrhoea did cause the pounds to simply fall off. That Christmas, not one item of magic underwear was required. The dress fitted her like a glove.

Admittedly, the doctors and nurses were a bit surprised she insisted on wearing it even in her hospital bed but, I suppose, if you have to spend Christmas Day hooked up to a saline drip, you might as well look spectacular.

"I bet you won't eat in that place again," I said to her when I visited.

"Don't be ridiculous, darling," she sniffed, "I've never felt so trim. What really annoys me is this: if I'd known I was going to lose so much weight so easily, I wouldn't have bothered attending that bloody slimming class."

I did suggest on this occasion, perhaps, she might want to

keep the dress. I thought – as the doctors indicated she should be home by then – she could wear it to attend her sister's annual New Year's Eve party.

"But I've been sick all down the front," she whined.

"No matter," I reasoned. "Since every year your sister's do is a bad-taste fancy dress event, it could be the perfect outfit."

My wife gave me what is best described as an icy stare.

I carried on regardless. "There's always a Hitler; or a guy with a shirt pulled over his head and a pumpkin under his arm, posing as a guillotine victim; or someone clutching a string of sausages to their belly pretending to be disembowelled. However, I bet no one has ever gone with genuine vomit plastered all over their costume."

The icy stare became, if possible, even icier.

At my wife's instruction, I spent all Boxing Day scouring the internet for a good specialist dry cleaner.

December 21st

Preparing Christmas Dinner

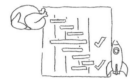

How could you hope to get roast turkey, chestnut stuffing, piggies-in-blankets, roast potatoes, red cabbage, parsnips (baked in a coating of black pepper and parmesan, please), sprouts (with pancetta and chestnuts) and giblet gravy - because that's the Christmas Dinner my lot expects - all on the table at the right time without a project plan?

Not to mention two choices of starter before the main meal. Which, depending on the particular members of the tribe coming, must include a gluten-free and a vegetarian option. Plus, the Christmas pudding and at least three alternatives to follow. Oh, of course, there had also better be custard, brandy cream, or ice-cream as accompaniments for each of the desserts. Cheese and biscuits followed by coffee and mints are, naturally, also taken as read.

So, yes, I do need a project plan. And, though I say it myself, my *Preparing Christmas Dinner* project plan is something wonderful to behold. Running to four pages, it lists all the required ingredients; what items must be taken out of the freezer the night before to defrost; which utensils I'll need; what pans I'll use for cooking what; oven temperature and timings; and even at what point I can find five minutes to slip upstairs to change out of my cook's scrubs into my Christmas outfit.

Over the years my plan (which I print out and stick to the fridge door for ease of consultation) has been mocked mercilessly by my children.

"Wow, Dad, this looks like a NASA project plan for a moon landing! Surely, after all these years, you don't need a plan? You make the same meal every Christmas."

"No, I don't," I patiently explain. "Dependent on who's coming, the size of the turkey changes as does the amount of vegetables. Ipso facto, cooking times alter. Not to mention the hour at which we eat. You have children of your own now and we have to fit dinner around their nap times. So, accordingly, I have to update my plan every year."

"Whatever," they smile dismissively. Their generation prefers to 'freestyle' everything, they tell me.

The annual revision of my project plan normally takes me a good couple of hours, sat at the computer each Christmas Eve morning.

Alas, last year disaster struck. Halfway through editing we

had a brief power cut. My computer died instantly. And though it did reboot quickly, as current was restored, when it came back, I discovered all my amendments were lost. Nor would the blasted original of my plan open. Nor would either of my two backups. I came very close to a heart attack.

"Surely, after all these years, you don't need a plan?" commented my wife.

I didn't bother going through all the rationale again.

"Search the internet, then," she suggested, "I'll bet someone will have posted one that serves just a well."

"You can't just use any old project plan," I insisted.

"You'll have to 'freestyle' it, then, won't you?" she unhelpfully concluded.

That was too horrible a thought to entertain. I decided, perhaps, it was worthwhile at least having a quick look on the internet.

What an astonishing resource the internet is. Within minutes I had found a 'Teach Yourself Project Planning' site with several sample plans, demonstrating how a project planning approach could be used to address a multiplicity of issues. Wonderfully, one was labelled *Christmas Dinner*. Ironically enough, it sat in the list just below one labelled *NASA Moonshot*.

I clicked the link and set off a download followed by an automatic close down of the computer, then headed for bed. The plan might not be as detailed as mine, but it was better than nothing.

Next morning, up early as usual, after half an hour in the kitchen conducting my *mise en place*, I went upstairs to my study and retrieved the plan from the printer. It was only then I realised I had clicked the wrong link. I'd mistakenly downloaded the one outlining the steps in a *NASA Moonshot*. There wasn't time to boot up the pc and try to find the site again. I would be forced to 'freestyle' it, after all.

Naturally, this was the cause of much hilarity in my family. They watched, full of amusement, as I began to clash pots about, hoping memory would serve well enough for me to muddle through. No doubt assuming it was the cream of the jest, they taped the *NASA Moonshot* plan up on the fridge, just in case it gave me inspiration.

Oddly, I think it must have. For, as I placed the turkey on the table for carving, more than one person commented how it had somehow developed a rather rocket-shaped anatomy. Which must have had something to do with the fact, I think, that as I was wrapping the bird in foil, I happened to glance up and my attention was drawn to an illustration demonstrating the '*Orientation and Placement of the Earth Atmosphere Re-entry Shield*'. I can only conclude the diagram must have unconsciously influenced my foil wrapping technique.

They also enjoyed, they said, that I had stuck sparklers all over the surface of the Christmas Pudding, because it made it look like a communications satellite. I can't deny that had been a more conscious - albeit impromptu - decision. It was a style of decoration suggested to me by the logo on top of the plan, showing an orbiting space station against a galaxy of stars.

Amazingly, everyone said it was the best Christmas dinner for years and, honestly, I think they were right. So, daft though it might sound, I'm seriously considering using that *NASA Moonshot* project plan every year from now on.

December 22nd

Christmas Pudding

I ONLY EVER ATE Christmas Pudding the once. Never again. It wasn't the taste that put me off - rather the fact that it very nearly killed me.

The Christmas Pudding near-death incident was also, incidentally, what made my mother develop her extremely antagonistic attitude towards the entire medical profession.

I was ten years old. For a reason unclear to me now, that year Mother decided to make a traditional plum duff pudding. This involved introducing into the mixture a family heirloom: a rare (she claimed) silver sixpence from the pre-decimal age.

Whoever got the coin in their portion, Mother announced,

would have good fortune throughout the coming year.

Well, I was the lucky one, wasn't I?

Except when I say 'lucky', it depends on how you look at it. In fact, I didn't even realise my portion contained the sixpence until the blasted thing got stuck in my windpipe.

Because I used to gobble my food in those days, it slipped straight down the wrong way. You might well lay the blame at my own door, saying if you eat like a pig what can you expect? But I point the finger at my sister Julia. If I didn't clear my plate rapidly, she was wont to steal the best bits off it. Julia was the favoured one. Mum and Dad never checked her behaviour.

Immediately the silver sixpence got stuck, I started coughing and spluttering. On seeing my discomfiture, every member of the family promptly adopted their usual response to witnessing another's misfortune. They started laughing.

Very quickly I found myself gasping for breath. Still finding the whole thing wildly humorous, Mum, Dad and Julia took turns banging their fists on my back - a first-aid treatment that only served to lodge in the coin more firmly.

The three of them had reached the point of tears streaming down their eyes, before it struck them I was genuinely beginning to choke to death.

The laughter stopped abruptly. Julia, always the drama queen, began screaming: a hysterical response only cut short when Dad instinctively slapped her hard across the face.

Even in my oxygen-deprived state, I remember thinking, '*You'll regret that, Dad.*' For, when it comes to holding a grudge, Julia had (and, for sure, still has) longer recall than even an elephant.

I heard Mum scream, "Call an ambulance!" and Dad scream back, "There isn't time!" before he bundled us all out of the front door, threw me and my sister onto the back seat of the car, and then drove off at top speed towards the nearest Accident and Emergency Department.

Luckily, we hadn't travelled further than the street corner before Dad realised in the panic he'd left Mum behind. So, only having to reverse back a couple of hundred yards to pick her up didn't, thankfully, delay us too much.

Fortunately, as well, we didn't live that far away from the hospital since, by this point, I was beginning to turn blue.

Once we arrived there, the staff grasped the situation immediately. I was manhandled quickly onto a trolley and rushed frantically down the corridor to a cubicle.

Here a nurse forcibly held me down while, after a perfunctory burst of local anaesthetic spray, a young doctor furiously delved down my throat with a ridiculously large pair of forceps, pulled from a packet labelled *'To be used for urgent Caesarean deliveries only'*.

As he dragged the sixpence out, I greedily sucked in a wonderful lungful of air.

It was to be another six years before I experienced my first real sexual orgasm. However, even the wondrous surge of ecstasy I experienced on that occasion didn't quite compare with the emotional rush I felt at being able to suddenly breathe again.

Half an hour later, back in the car on the way home, with everyone calmer, Mum leaned over from the front seat and said to me, "Give me the sixpence. I don't think we'll use it in a pudding again."

"I haven't got it," I told her.

She obviously thought I was messing about but, recognising I'd just been through a bit of a trauma, decided not to shout at me.

"Come on," she said, "that coin is a very rare year, so it's worth a fair bit. Though it's not the monetary value. My Grandad carried it all through the First World War. It was his lucky charm."

"I thought your Grandad lost a leg in the war?"

"He did."

"And got gassed as well?"

"Yes, that's right."

"And didn't you tell me that he was shot in the arm too?"

"Yes, he was."

"And he reckoned that coin brought him good luck, did he?"

"Just give it to me," Mum snapped.

"Honestly," I said, "I haven't got it."

"Surely the doctor gave it to you? Don't say it was just left on the trolley?"

"It wasn't," Julia broke in. "I saw the doctor pick it up, stare at it, and smile."

"Smile?" my mother queried, "why would the doctor smile?"

"It looked to me as if he was checking the date," Julia said. "Then, after wiping it, he put it in his pocket, with an even bigger smile on his face."

This being a Christmas story, I think it best not to record the unchristian words my mother uttered at this point. That day, the medical profession fell from grace in her eyes. She was never to be civil to a doctor again.

December 23rd

Christmas Crackers

Someone really should sort out the rules. I mean, crackers are meant to be an amusing Christmas novelty - but not in our house, they're not!

Although I do love pulling a cracker, I get so apprehensive, every festive season, about how much domestic discord pulling them is going to bring. Before we go through it all again this year, there are some fundamental questions I really would welcome somebody answering.

For a start, do you have to offer your cracker to be pulled by the person sitting next to you? Is it mandatory? Or are you permitted to invite anyone in the vicinity to pull your cracker

- provided, of course, they can safely do it without knocking a wine glass over?

And, if the convention is that your cracker must be offered to the person next to you, is it customary to offer always it to the left (as with passing the port) or to the right?

Whichever it is, surely there has to be consistency? Because, if some people offer their cracker to the left and other people offer their cracker to the right - if you think about it - there's a very strong probability that someone won't get invited to pull a cracker at all.

And knowing my luck, that person would be me.

All this, of course, assumes you are pulling crackers sat at a table. But what if you're not? What if you're pulling each other's crackers as part of a buffet tea?

In such circumstances, should individuals be allowed to cross the room and invite whomsoever they please to pull their cracker? Because, if they do, won't the occasion simply degenerate into a vulgar publicity contest? Instead of people pairing-off, everyone will just rush over to the most-liked person in the room, brandishing their cracker at them.

In these circumstances there's also every likelihood that some unfortunate won't be offered anybody's cracker to pull.

Me, again, no doubt.

Why hasn't someone given authoritative guidance before now?

Perhaps they have and I'm just not aware of it. It's not impossible, I suppose that, unbeknownst to me, there is an official guide. Entitled, *The Etiquette of Cracker-Pulling,* perhaps? Well, if there is, can I, please, be informed of its ISBN number so I can order a copy.

Though, even if the question of who can offer their cracker to whom were to be satisfactorily resolved, that wouldn't be the end of the matter, would it? There's still the question of the right of ownership over a cracker's contents.

For, when you pull a cracker, it never rips dead centre. That's not the way it works. The laws of physics - or is it mechanics? - don't guarantee 'equivalence of outcome', as my Uncle Arthur once said to me (whatever that's supposed to mean).

Uncle Arthur was an engineer, so you'd think he'd know what he's talking about. However, he's also a notorious practical joker, so he might just have been pulling my leg.

Whatever, the blunt truth is, after a cracker has been pulled, one person ends up with the short half and one person ends up with the long half. And, generally, all things considered, it's the long half that contains the hat, the motto, and the novelty item.

But to whom should the hat, motto, and novelty item of a pulled cracker belong? Is it the person who ended up with the long half, or should it be the person who offered their cracker to be pulled in the first place?

I mean there's little skill involved in pulling a cracker. It largely comes down to brute strength. So other things being equal, it's generally bound to be the stronger person who ends up with the long half.

But if they just get to walk away with the hat, motto and novelty item every time, where's the morality in that? Isn't it just the law of the jungle?

It's merely a thought, but why don't the factories who make Christmas crackers prepare them with a ring of discreet perforations at the mid-point, to give those of us with weaker wrists at least a chance of winning?

This would certainly help me because, being one of Nature's weaklings, I never do well at cracker-pulling. I always end up with the short half. And when it was my cracker that's just been pulled, I have to resort to begging to be handed the hat, motto and novelty item which, in my opinion, should be rightfully mine.

Oh, and talking of the novelty items that come out of crackers, I'd like someone to lay down the law regarding swapping. Are we, as a society, for it or against?

I'll lay my cards on the table: I'm in favour of it. Though, I have to add this rider: if there is to be swopping, it must be open and above board. There has to be full public scrutiny. Because, in my experience, if there isn't total transparency, all sorts of skullduggery start to occur.

Let me share a case in point. Last year my Uncle Arthur (he of the 'equivalence of outcome statement') got, from his cracker, an amusing magic trick in the form of an interlocked pair of steel rings while, from mine (after begging – see above) I got a plastic whistle.

I knew for certain that Uncle Arthur had got exactly the same magic trick the year before. So why would he want to keep it? But when I asked him to swop, he outright refused.

"What do I want with a crummy plastic whistle?" he said. "I bet it doesn't even blow."

Well, he was wrong there. It did blow. Not very well, admittedly. You couldn't referee a football match, or start a train, with it, that's true. But Uncle Arthur was wrong, that whistle did blow.

Yet, despite disdaining my whistle, I later found out that he had secretly swapped his magic trick for the keyring my brother had got from his cracker.

Now, where was the fairness in that? How was my brother's keyring any better than my whistle? Even if my whistle was a crummy plastic one, his keyring was crummy plastic too.

All of this, I realise, boils down to one fundamental philosophical question: whether pulling crackers should be seen as a contest - a straightforward, all-or-nothing adversarial battle, where one party wins and the other party loses – or, instead, a communal endeavour, to be undertaken by a social group in a spirit of mutual cooperation, with the explicit aim of promoting collective pleasure, harmony and wellbeing?

It's such a desperately important issue. I need it resolving for, as I've already intimated, in our family, since we're not all playing to the same set of rules, every year cracker-pulling descends into the most unseemly squabble. Which I, generally, don't do well out of.

Look don't misunderstand me, I don't think for one minute crackers shouldn't be pulled. Just pulled fairly.

And neither am I advocating that all the hats, mottoes, and novelties should simply be pooled on the table, and people be allowed to take their pick.

I'm not a Marxist.

I just want an end to anarchy.

Christmas Eve

The Big Tin of Sweets

When it comes to the big day, naturally, for dinner you want your turkey and cranberry sauce, your brussel sprouts, your piggies-in-blankets, your parsnips, and your roast potatoes. With, to follow of course, Christmas pudding and brandy sauce.

Let's be honest, though. Traditional and tasty as those things are, what you truly look forward to is the moment when dinner is done, and you can finally open the big tin of sweets.

That big tin may be Quality Street, or Roses, or Heroes, or Celebrations, or even, if you're lucky, all four of them.

Once upon a time, of course, the big tin of sweets was

genuinely made of real tin. A solid piece of kit that later could be used for the storage of all manner of domestic bits and bobs.

What's more, the sweets they contained had proper old-fashioned wrappers, made of coloured cellophane and foil. Wrappers that had to be untwisted, rather than just ripped open. Wrappers that, once you'd eaten the sweets inside, provided wonderful opportunities for beginner origami.

Those were the good old days. Now, the 'tins' are made of plastic and the wrappings don't have quite the same class.

However, even if now plastic, that container sitting under the Christmas tree still tantalises with its presence. Every time you look at it, you can't help wondering, *could I get the top off and steal a couple of my favourites without anyone noticing?*

But no chance of that with modern packaging. In the past, the tin lid was secured with a strip of sticky tape that, with care, you could peel back and, after pinching a sweet, carefully reapply, with no one being the wiser. But, in these plastic days, once the seal on the container is broken, that's it. Everybody would know you've been dipping your fingers in.

Just another thing altered by the relentless march of time. Nothing is what it used to be.

So, the modern, tamper-proof, container must sit there untouched and awaiting its proper moment. The very embodiment of deferred gratification. Which is rather ridiculous, when you think about it. Supermarket promotions being so competitive, with prices so heavily discounted in the run-up to Christmas, you could buy yourself a tin every single week and gorge the lot, if you chose to.

Though, really, where would be the pleasure in that? As

someone famous once said, "Half of the pleasure in any great pleasure is in the very pleasant pleasure of pleasantly anticipating that great pleasure".

Was it someone famous who said that? Or was it actually my dad? Because he did have a habit, in his cups, of coming out with that kind of tripe.

Of course, the most significant reason for leaving the big tin of sweets untouched until Christmas Day is the well-known, though inexplicable, fact that sweets eaten before then somehow don't taste quite right. I, personally, am convinced that, like a fine wine, after manufacture and packing, the sweets continue to mature inside their wrappers. Only reaching their absolute point of perfection at precisely midday on December 25th.

It is also a self-evident truth that the big tin of sweets is a better experience for not being consumed alone. Consumed alone, a big tin of sweets is just one more step towards diabetes; eaten in company, it becomes a profound exercise in human bonding.

Oh, that magical moment when, at last, the time arrives for the seal to be broken and the family to dive in.

Pandora's Box did not hold such wonders. It is like looking at a pirate chest full of treasure. Round hard toffees; barrel-shaped gooey toffees; half-moon shaped caramels; conical caramels containing a nut; octagonal orange crisps; chocolate domes full of honeycomb; square slabs of chocolate crammed with fondants of all flavours known to man. There is surely a sweet for everyone and, for everyone, a particular sweet.

Except, hiding in every tin is one unfathomable mystery. But an unfathomable mystery only to be revealed in the fullness of time.

Probably every family has its own particular time-honoured rituals for how the after-dinner sweet eating should be undertaken. Unwritten rules governing the competition for securing your favourites and delineating what is considered fair gameplay, and what downright chicanery.

For example, in our house, the sweet tin passes from oldest to youngest. As it circulates, only the one sweet may be taken at a time. It is also considered shockingly bad form for an individual to choose exactly the same type of sweet on every rotation.

However, this rule of 'no recurrent identical sweet picking' obtains only while participants are physically in the room. If anyone leaves, perhaps to take a lavatory break, then all bets are off. In our family it's crucial to make sure you've done your business and got comfortable before the big tin of sweets gets opened.

Whatever process you and your kin adopt, one by glorious one the wrappers are ripped off and the gorgeous confectionery is scoffed. Until, at last, that unfathomable mystery referred to above finally presents itself.

Eventually, there will be just one sweet rolling round an otherwise empty tin. One last sweet which, no matter how many times the tin is passed, and no matter how hard others are pressed to take it, remains unpicked, unwanted and alone. The one sweet which no one is willing to eat.

Ah, you've discovered it. That conundrum of the confectionery world: your particular family's *Universally Despised Flavour.*

Christmas Day

After Hard Labour, Even the Gods Must Rest

Coming home
After a long night on the sleigh,
I go into a solitary room
To remove my breeches,
Shirt and headgear,
Which I seal up tightly in a bag
For Mrs. Claus to wash.

Keeping a peg
Clipped tight over my nose,
My pants and shirt
I throw into the stove:
They are quite beyond redemption.

Next door,
My wife has drawn a bath,
With oils and unguents,
Frankincense and myrrh,
In which I soak
My freezing, aching bones.

Until I'm soaped
And every inch is sponged,
And smelling once more unrepellant,
The peg stays on.

For, even if it is
The sweat
Of a still delightful labour,
I have no desire
To experience the smell
Of my own personal petrichor.

Twelfth Night (And Far Beyond)

The Last Piece of Christmas Glitter

After taking down the Christmas cards, I assiduously hoovered the carpet. Even so, afterwards I found shards of glitter.

Over the next few days, I found it in my hair, under my nails, and stuck to many of my clothes.

Christmas glitter gets sodding everywhere.

I realised, to free myself of it, I would have to mount a campaign.

Accordingly, I washed my hair, scrubbed my hands, and put my clothes through the most rigorous washing cycle of which my machine is capable.

Then I did it all again.

In addition, I rented an industrial vacuum cleaner and traversed every surface of the house, inch by painstaking inch.

Then I did it again.

Next day, despite realising I was indulging in total overkill, I did all of these things yet one more time. Once completed, I felt able to congratulate myself that - absolutely and definitely - I had removed every last microscopic dot of shiny plastic shed by those Christmas cards.

Hoorah! All the glitter was gone.

I lived in my fool's paradise for maybe a week.

Then, this morning after showering, I reached into a drawer to get a clean pair of underpants and - horror of horrors - as I put in my first leg, I saw it. Hiding deep down inside a seam. One still surviving shard of bright silver glitter.

Like a tiny eye.

A tiny eye which, I could have sworn, was brazenly winking at me.

About The Author

PHIL IS REPORTEDLY THE figment of someone's imagination.

He is not.

Let's face it, if someone had imagined him, they would have imagined a person much taller and a lot more handsome.

A person easier to sum up too.

I mean has he had an erratic trajectory through life, or what?

At different times, Phil has worked in the NHS, the music business, theatre, radio and – though, admittedly, only for one day – been lead singer on a musical tour of launderettes.

Perhaps the only note of constancy through all this has been his very over-developed sense of the ridiculous.

Though he's had many pieces published in anthologies, this is Phil's first complete book under his own name (if it's not an assumed one, that is).

Printed in Great Britain
by Amazon